SOLANA IN A NUTSHELL

THE DEFINITIVE GUIDE TO ENTER THE WORLD
OF DECENTRALIZED FINANCE, LENDING, YIELD
FARMING, DAPPS AND MASTER IT COMPLETELY

SEBASTIAN ANDRES

WB PUBLISHING

CONTENTS

HOW TO USE THE BOOK

How to use the book

First of all I would like to thank you for your trust and for choosing me as your guide to embark on this journey into the world of Cryptocurrencies. This book will help you to understand and master this world with the objective of obtaining an excellent financial education through the comprehension and understanding of Cryptocurrencies. In this book we will go from the most basic to the most advanced.

We understand that entering the world of cryptocurrencies can be tedious and very slow because there is a lot of information that we must understand and assimilate, usually the pioneers in this type of technology are people who have no problem to generate passive income online because they have some basic knowledge of this world that can help them a lot. The purpose of this book is that you can also shorten this path and have the knowledge in time to take advantage of them, as you know the world of cryptocurrencies moves very quickly and you can not waste time.

This technology is here to stay and to give us, the ordinary people, more economic and financial freedom.

In my experience, one of the things that caught my attention when I became interested in cryptocurrencies back in 2011, was the concept of freedom that is related to currencies such as Bitcoin, Monero, Dash, Zcash, etc. where the control of the whole process always goes by hand with the user because of the privacy they provide. Don't worry, you will understand these concepts later on during the development of the book.

In this book I will teach you the different approaches to Cryptocurrencies and the technology behind it: starting from the actual concept of money to the Blockchain, why it works, what is the secret behind it and we will also debunk some myths related to some concepts.

The objective of this book is to teach you to have a more complete and complex notion about Cryptocurrencies, from the most basic concepts such as knowing how everything works, how the pieces fit together, to the most advanced.

I have also taken the time to suggest some resources to get you started on the right foot. Keep in mind that many of these links are affiliate links, so you will receive some discounts and benefits by using the referred link, at no cost to you. So take advantage of it.

I wrote this book not only to inform you about the world of cryptocurrencies but also to motivate you to take that step that is so hard for you and take action, that is why I want to ask you one thing, do not give up throughout this book, follow the advice at your own risk, I promise you that by finishing this book and applying step by step my advice and teachings you will be able to better understand this world and according to your personal actions achieve financial freedom or also support this initiative that gives power to us citizens against the current financial system that is too manipulated and makes a few people rich.

Again, thank you very much for purchasing this book, I hope you enjoy it.

ABOUT ME

Why should you listen to me?

Greetings, my name is Sebastian Andres, I am an entrepreneur, writer and world traveler. I am a cryptocurrency enthusiast since 2011 when I started to get interested in this world. I feel extremely blessed to have been born in this era, and to be able to experience the growth of these technologies such as the internet and cryptocurrencies.

For more than 10 years I have focused on developing several internet businesses, which taught me to develop my own strategies and methods to generate passive income. Cryptocurrencies was one of them and that is how I achieved financial freedom.

The purpose of my books, more specifically of the collection "Cryptocurrency Basics" (in which I bring the most current and reliable information on cryptocurrencies, if you are interested you can look for the other books in this collection, in which we address other cryptos) is to be a source of inspiration for you and generate a change in those who are not satisfied with the established and know that they can give more, that they can generate a positive change in their lives and get to design that lifestyle they want so much.

I am confident that this information will help you to get that final jump start and get into cryptocurrencies in depth.

DISCLAIMER

Important

Investing in financial markets such as cryptocurrencies and other assets can lead to money losses. The purpose of this book is only educational and does not represent an investment advice, for that there are already many professionals in the area that can help you. Proceed with caution, at your own risk and remember, never invest more than you are willing to lose.

By continuing to read this book you accept this Warning.

1

UNDERSTANDING HOW SOLANA WORKS AND WHY IT IS SO REVOLUTIONARY

Every day that passes, every second that the online economic network makes its characteristic movements, we see how digital or electronic money; which we call and currently known as cryptocurrencies, the representation of an important asset that is based and supported by cryptographic encryption systems, allowing its holders a sustainable and proven guarantee of legitimate ownership; is gaining more and more ground in the field of negotiations at all levels.

A trend in a new format that is gaining significant preponderance and growth at every moment and that little by little is becoming present in family, youth and business economies; it is reaching previously unimagined levels and is moving the world in a way that even the creators of these virtual currencies had not considered. Referring to the number of cryptocurrencies emerged and how many remain after their appearance in the market, capitalizing and rising in position trying to reach the first places and move with all energy among the almost 9,000 existing cryptocurrencies or the more than 4,000 accounted for the month of August 2021.

Achieving important positions such as being among the first 1,000, the first 100 or the first 10, is not easy at all. Only the structure of the currency itself, its configuration, format, value, movement, capitalization, security and trust, will be responsible for making a cryptocurrency present, strong and stable, that no matter how old it is, knows how to move with skill and ability inside and outside the network, making itself always present.

An important case and example of the former expressed in this project that you are beginning to read today, is represented by Solana (SOL). A cryptocurrency conceived and work devised in the year 2017, officially and operationally launched to the market during the month of March 2020 by the Solana Foundation, based in Geneva (Switzerland), which, in the midst of a global pandemic crisis, generated by the COVID-19, is positioned against all odds, during the month of October 2021, in the number 6 position, behind Cardano (ADA) and close enough to Ethereum (ETH) and the powerful Bitcoin (BTC). By the early hours of the day on October 28, 2021, Solana (SOL) already had a price of US195.86 and a capitalization of over US$58.9 billion.

The name given to this cryptocurrency is Solana (SOL), referring from its name to the well-known coastal town of Solana Beach, located in the northern part of San Diego, Calif. United States. Probably its creators, who stand out as excellent surfers, did honor to their nascent digital currency, baptizing it as Solana, a place of predilection for their moments of relaxation and fun; adrenaline, strength and height on the waves in their favorite west coast.

Thanks to his initiative, creativity and knowledge, Anatoly Yakovenko, a graduate in Computer Science, who worked as a software engineer for Dropbox, as well as for D2iQ, former Mesosphere and was Senior Staff Engineer Manager at Qualcomm, and who joined two of his best friends and notable colleagues: Greg Fitzgerald and Stephen Akridge, conceived, created and materialized his own cryptocurrency giving it the name Solana (SOL), and for which the White Paper was published in 2017. Thus, they formalized in this way and placing to public light of the network market, a year later, in 2018; their own Blockchain prototype, based on that book. Designed, made and structured according to the guidelines and requirements inherent to the dynamics for the purposes and purposes that this project deserves and deserves.

The project and the Solana (SOL) cryptocurrency, has its physical headquarters in the European continent, specifically established in the city of Geneva, Switzerland and has its technological foundations in the aforementioned White Book of its creator, Anatoly Yakovenko. In due course, Yakovenko stated in a confident and decisive manner, that thanks to the new and unprecedented Blockchain architecture model supported in the "Proof-Of-History" (PoH) format, created and presented by Anatoly in 2017; there would be a valuable Blockchain algorithmic element that would act as a fundamental complementary method and process to the well-known and put into practice "Proof-Of-Stake" (PoS). As a result of this consensus method, it was sought to speed up and consolidate the processes, providing them with a resource that would allow them the fair codification and optimal use of the Blockchain time itself and its constant mobility in the network.

Yakovenko and his team dedicated significant periods of analysis and study to the operation, performance, profitability, mobility, etc. Which, by the end of the second decade of the present century, represented and characterized the most known and most moved cryptocurrencies by then. Seeing a growing cryptographic market that, in the face of all economic adversity faced by the different nations and great powers, which, in its own stock market and mercantile philosophy, seeks to satisfy needs in favor of its communities, guaranteeing resources according to the possibilities of the moment, inspires the trio to behave like the salmon, which against the current manages to reach the goal.

Thus, the Solana protocol (SOL); emerges as a new alternative with aspirations to achieve wonderful results and that to the proof we can observe and find, in only one year and seven months of its launching, in the Top 10 of the most important electronic currencies in the world, defending the position number 6; looking strong and powerful next to the until today unbeatable Cardano ADA in the number 5 position, Tether USDT in the number 4 position, Binance Coin BNB in the number 3 position, Ethereum ETH in the number 2 position and the powerful Bitcoin BTC in the number 1 position, which against all odds tries to maintain firm, stable and able to do whatever is necessary to meet the expectations of its community.

An aspect that serves as a reference with its pros and cons to this and many other projects, is precisely the case of Ethereum ETH, a cryptocurrency that was born on the basis of a set of weaknesses or areas of opportunity that the young writer and programmer of Russian origin, born in 1994, Vitálik Buterin saw in Bitcoin BTC and sought to correct in favor of this and that did not have the expected receptivity or viable support.

Buterin's determination and conviction that it was possible to verify "something" was not only a concern that, had it materialized, would have favored Bitcoin BTC; it moved to a point of no return in the decision to, also with his experience as a video gamer, make himself felt and give a big change to the crypto world with the creation of his own currency: Ethereum ETH. This today continues to make history. Facts like these and many others, add to our list of great projects and ventures, capable of transforming economies around the world, providing new growth options.

Solana (SOL) was created with very clear visions, aims, plans, intentions, objectives and purposes, defined and in accordance with its unique personality as an original and genuine cryptocurrency with sufficiently particular supports in its credit and property. Which we will know progressively and in a friendly and manageable way, understanding in this way, not only the basic standard operation of

Solana (SOL), but its structure and the best way to identify ourselves with it to manage it, not only for the robustness it obtains every day, in its price or capitalization; also, for the benefits, security and guarantee of seriousness and reliability.

Continuing with characteristic details of the way Solana (SOL) opens to the cryptographic market and its operative power; we mention the capacity that this cryptocurrency has of being a cryptocurrency with the capacity to resist about 55,000 transactions per second. We are talking about a Blockchain with Decentralized Applications (DApps), as one of the most important cases of the network. As practitioners and active participants of the crypto market, or followers of a new and relevant market trend, we have had the opportunity to see how these Decentralized Applications (DApps) have been constantly evolving and developing, generating from games such as the well-known CryptoKitties, to the point of generating or becoming the basis and support of Decentralized Finance (DeFi).

To talk about Solana (SOL) is not only to say that it is a Blockchain that enjoys an amazing capacity and great support in number of transactions per second; we are referring to a Blockchain very well analyzed in its creation to be of exclusivity of Decentralized Applications (DApps), seeking to become a crypto alternative to Ethereum (ETH), and why, for allowing, thanks to its software; to avoid congesting the network against a high number of operations, procedures or transactions per second. It is therefore an aspect with great value that Solana (SOL) possesses and that is in full power to support the cryptographic ecosystem.

Solana (SOL) is a new or next generation Blockchain transformational crypto-economic project or plan, which is based on an opensource system with a fascinating and important enough purpose for the network, and that is to give a proper impulse to the development of Decentralized Applications (DApps) for the next and coming generations. If we give the qualifier of scalability to Solana (SOL), it is because it is in the sure search to make available to the system its scalable platform with great guarantees and clear possibilities of decentralization. In addition, we must add to the above; the fact that Solana (SOL) also seeks to have thousands of nodes in order to avoid the use of high-cost hardware which, in turn, results in high consumption in energy levels.

The development of Solana (SOL) has started and taken its first steps from scratch, thus allowing an interesting approach to its particular scalable feature. The purpose of its developers is to make it understood that by achieving an adequate combination of diverse algorithms that give rise to a Blockchain, it has the ability to reduce the difficulties that usually occur in the network due to high saturation conflicts. It is here and with Solana (SOL), that it is possible to obtain a network with high performance standards, even when the number of transactions is very high.

What is Solana? What is so special about Solana?

Solana (SOL), as already mentioned, is a cryptocurrency that appears on the network as a financial option or economic resource added to the current virtual demand that demands more and new alternatives that fit its conditions and that, in neuroscience, resembles the market and people. It is an open-source protocol, a project conceived, created and designed by Anatoly Yakovenko, with the idea and intention to facilitate and make more and more friendly the creation of the already known dApps, Decentralized Applications. Solana (SOL), a high-end functional protocol, is also based on the decentralized, free or independent ecosystem that characterizes Blockchain technology. All this leads to the generation of excellent DeFi, Decentralized Financial solutions.

Thanks to the agreement, which under hybrid consensus is generated through the Blockchain network, today Solana (SOL) has gained the interest and attention of entrepreneurs and small traders, as well as large companies, institutions and organizations of high spectrum. From this point, it is of vital importance for the Solana Foundation and center of attention, to achieve that the decentralized financial and mercantile activity, reaches a greater accessibility after an increasing scale or level. Thus, and by means of this dynamic; it is viable a scalability of protocol each time greater, increasing in this way its use and utility.

Every project carries with it a series of vital aspects in favor of its feasibility, and within this series of points, the objectives are fundamental. Solana (SOL) considers the scalability and adaptability of negotiations as a primary objective, through the introduction or insertion of the "Proof-Of-History" (PoH) consensus in conjunction with the "Proof-Of-Stakes" (PoS), which comes from the Blockchain.

It is there where lies a very particular and, moreover, special enough quality that has and characterizes Solana (SOL), making it stand out from the many other cryptocurrencies; and it is to carry with it a tool of its own formative protocol, and it is the consensus of "Proof-Of-History" (Proof-Of-History - PoH), created by Yakovenko. PoH, by its acronym, is an interesting and favorable algorithm of complete and integral benefit that has the ability to facilitate its optimal and friendly use of the platform, offering in addition to security; all the necessary confidence for its users and holders of this novel cryptocurrency.

Another particular differential that makes Solana (SOL) a truly special cryptocurrency, is to be known inside and outside the cryptographic ecosystem, with another great variant represented by its fast, short and immediate times during the process in their procedures and negotiations, which are really short, thanks to the offer or goodness that provides its Blockchain or blockchain, duly endorsed to the most accurate and timely protocols; able to provide immediate response to a procedure that deserves and requires it.

It is important to always keep in mind and take into account what we are talking about and/or knowing a cryptocurrency, which is not at all exempt or free from volatility or unpredictability. Like any other digital currency, Solana (SOL) carries with it the quality of investment susceptible to risks and economic trances at any time, even more so in relation to the daily market activity or behavior of other cryptocurrencies that undoubtedly and by historical knowledge, is evident in the network. Solana (SOL) is a practically debutant cryptocurrency, and although less popular than Cardano ADA, Shiba INU or Dogecoin DOGE; it has been highly benefited with the behavior of its advance towards the first 10 positions among the most important and outstanding coins of the virtual market. This is demonstrated by its current quotation value, as well as its positioning in active and progressive capitalization.

Solana (SOL) is and represents for its clients, followers and the entire market, trust and support. A clear example of this is the strong connection failure that occurred on September 14, 2021, a day in which the cryptocurrency remained out of service for an estimated 17 hours, with its servers interrupted and operations suspended. Although in less than 24 hours Solana's (SOL) operational service was fully restored; no losses of funds were recorded across its entire spectrum.

The serious and responsible response given by the organization about this strange event was clarified hours later, notifying the affected community and in general that the cause responsible for such a blockage was due to a "denial of service attack". It happened that around 12:00UTC, Grape Protocol, a decentralized Social Networking system for crypto communities, developed by Solana, launched its IDO in Raydium, but the bots in its system caused a high number of transactions that, for some reason, collapsed the network, flooding its platform and leaving it inoperative, due to excess and overload in the web circulation channel.

With the resolution of this event, and even more the guarantee of funds completely protected and without negative consequences, the robustness of software and other protocols that act and are developed in favor of Solana (SOL), supported by a professional multidisciplinary team of programmers and engineers around the world, who the following 14 hours after the incident, worked together to achieve the total solution of updating and full restart of the network between a little more than 1,000 dedicated validators.

Solana (SOL), comes to life thanks to a project empowered and developed by Solana Labs, founded as we already know, in 2017 by Anatoly Yakovenko, who kept the premise of creating a novel verification system for transactions called "Proof-Of-History" (PoH), which gives the network the ability to withstand thousands of transactions per second.

The necessary self-management of financing was only possible after the launch of an Initial Coin Offering (ICO), which raised an impressive 26 million US dollars. It is important to note that by the beginning of 2020, and in the face of a COVID-19 Coronavirus pandemic, which began to close doors, windows and access to the physical world, the official launch of Solana (SOL) took place, which, operating under the beta scheme, fulfills and plays a role of valuable utility, as well as recognition in the cryptographic world.

Like all existing digital currencies, Solana (SOL) has its own native cryptocurrency identified as SOL, which functions as a very useful token. We will talk about it and its details later.

For the moment, let's highlight what continues to make Solana (SOL) different and special among the many and diverse existing cryptos, taking into consideration its growth and positioning among the first 10 most relevant and relevant currencies in the world, occupying to date the number 6 position with all firmness and the possibility of achieving a rise both in position and in price and capitalization.

The organization strives to promote inside and outside the market, its most important and relevant differentiating element; selling itself as the cryptocurrency that has the fastest and fastest growing Blockchain in the world. In addition, the Solana (SOL) project enjoys a sufficiently exclusive privilege; consolidating itself as the base and floor of more than 400 projects for the purchase and sale of Non Fungible Token (NFT) and also for Decentralized Finance (DeFi), the two main and most relevant trends within the cryptographic environment for online exchanges around the world.

Undoubtedly, it must be recognized that the Solana (SOL) project represents an innovative alternative, thanks to its hybrid consensus which allows the significant reduction of validation process times, applicable to each and every transaction as well as to the execution or activation of Smart Contracts.

Its timed periods of time are effectively fast, which arouses great interest in the entire virtual community such as government institutions, private, small and medium enterprises; as well as traders, small investors and the community in general. Solana (SOL), comes to satisfy a great need of effectiveness in the cryptographic market processes, in favor of those who make mercantile, financial and business life through a digital currency that gathers the best and most appropriate feasible and effective operative characteristics.

Among the multiple benefits and economic advantages that Solana (SOL) offers to its cyber-investors, is the fact that there are no increases or increases in tariffs or taxes for services. This important platform has been meticulously conceived in such a way that its operating costs are as low as possible in terms of transaction and that it is also committed to guaranteeing sustainable and reliable scalability over time, with effectively fast processing, at the pace required by the community and the system.

The widely demonstrated and proven experience enjoyed by its creators, Greg Fitzgerald and Anatoly Yakovenko; mainly, who for a long time have been part of valuable technological work teams in software development and other computational processes, have immediately endorsed it; have immediately endorsed a high level of recognition to Solana (SOL), allowing it to climb relevant positions compared to other coins of many years in the industry, such is the case of its location in the ranking of best coins by CoinMarketCap, rising from 22nd place in the month of February 2021, to the position in the month of October of the same year. A growth that admires its loyal followers, surprises the market and excites investors.

That has been the beginning of Solana (SOL), full of satisfactions; after moments of hard work, compromising and not easy at all, because achieving from a minimum expression, positions, references and trends of so much value; is only won with determination, commitment and dedication, complying with the philosophy of conception and creation of a new cryptocurrency that remains unstoppable. This is what makes Solana (SOL) special.

What are Solana (SOL) tokens?

First of all, let's start by defining and specifying that a token is the unitary representation that a certain organization creates, founds or establishes as an element of value to govern its own business model, and in this way grant much more power to its users, thus being able to enjoy an adequate interaction with the effects and resources, since it makes them more viable and practical the time required in favor of its participants and supports them in the commercialization and marketing with important benefits for the benefit of all the shareholders that make mercantile life in the network.

A "Token" is simply, in other words, a simple and new word within the glossary of words found in the crypto-mercantile culture, which represents a unit of value that is issued by and on behalf of a private financial entity. Graphically, and so that we have a more precise and material idea of what a Token is, let's see the tokens that are used in the mechanical parks to enjoy the attractions; this is what a Token looks like.

For example, a token has a special and very close relationship of similarity with Bitcoin (BTC); since it is given and receives a value that is approved and accepted by consensus by its community of participants and is established in its own Blockchain. The token may well be even more extensive and developed, broader. It can be over-valued more than a currency itself, given that a token, however simple in value it may be or represent, has an infinite number of uses, considering that they are based on a Blockchain protocol.

About the Solana Tokens (SOL), it is estimated that there are approximately 260 million Tokens being part of the most prominent platforms for exchanges, existing in the world, and despite the fact that the valuations estimated by the Solana Foundation, whose head-quarters is established in Switzerland, carefully guiding the movements of this cryptocurrency, is that an average of 489 million of these Tokens are produced and launched to the market.

According to the dynamics, sharp movements, ups and downs and alternate successions that support the most popular cryptocurrencies in their prices and values, due to certain regulations, make other tokens such as Solana (SOL), called alternative tokens, capture a high level of attention in the market.

A few weeks ago, in China it was declared that any type of transaction, negotiation or procedure with digital currencies is completely illegal; in this country they continue to study how to incorporate the digital yuan to the crypto-currency market, an event that, for example, had a negative impact on Bitcoin (BTC); generating a very sharp and strong fall.

By the first week of September, more precisely on the 5th of this month, the Solana Token (SOL) tripled in value over a period of three weeks, surpassing its market value by more than 41 billion US dollars. By that time Solana (SOL) reached the number 7 spot among the top ten most popular coins on the network, the largest in the world. All this was happening while it was beginning to be considered in an optimistic environment, the possibility given to the blockchain or Blockchain of Solana (SOL), as a strong competitor in a time perhaps not very close, but sure, against Ethereum (ETH), a neighbor close enough on the leaderboard.

Those who defend and support the Solana (SOL) project, are dedicated to disseminate and publicize its powerful feature of great speed, as well as the low cost in its transactions and operations in Decentralized Finance (Decentralized Finance - DeFi) and chargeable online, Apps in which the main domain seems to be in the hands of Ethereum (ETH).

Below, we share the opinion of an expert in crypto-assets. Antoni Trenchev, who is co-founder of the renowned Nexo Bank Crypto, and said, "Solana has a growing ecosystem, projects are being built on it and it has benefited greatly from the way they are looking at NFTs." Recall that NFTs are Non-Fungible Tokens (NFTs) that are handled in trading or better-known exchanges of virtual cashable assets.

Let's not forget that the Solana (SOL) platform or project is a "Proof-Of-Stake" (PoS) network, which has the outstanding possibility of designating its tokens to the freely selected validator. These validators are responsible for processing transactions and running the network, performing this activity in an optimal, efficient, timely and effective manner; they receive their appropriate and fair reward.

It is important to know that these validators are selected or chosen in function or according to the function in the amount that represents their participation that the validator has in the network. Every participant who owns Solana Tokens (SOL), has the freedom to assign his Tokens to a specific validator so that this in turn, perform the transfer or complete the operation of the holder, through Staking (bets) and thus obtain more profits or rewards.

In this process, the user who delegates his tokens is obliged to pay the validator the corresponding commission, representative of the percentage in favor of the rewards received. It is a dynamic of knowing how to apply the "Win-Win" formula or expression. With this we can clearly see and understand that Tokens are a solution designed, created and planned to allow its users a use that guarantees benefits resulting from a commercial activity of exchange.

A Non Fungible Token (NFT) is a cryptographic token that has the advantage of being genuine, unrepeatable and unique. It has the faculty of indivisibility and total legitimacy. It cannot be divided or fractioned. It has the preeminence of being able to represent elements of the physical world, tangible material; as well as virtual objects with the same characteristic features.

At the end of October 2021, the representative prices of Solana Tokens (SOL), rebounded in a unique and forceful way; to the point of reaching relevant records, mainly in the United States markets.

The Solana Token, and native to this platform, has been a great performer, practically throughout the course of the year 2021. The SOL token has benefited from the mimetic function, that is to say, everything that shows a good performance and meets the public's expectations, satisfying needs and works properly while there are uptrend situations, will be what the consumer will ultimately look for. What stands out and holds firm in unstable times, or better yet, acquires more value in times of turbulence, will be what they will look for and want to buy.

Today, and just as we are researching and writing these lines, SOL is consolidated as one of the tokens with the highest levels of negotiation in centralized exchanges. These have been executed and are most commonly found in the very popular and well known Coinbase and Binance transactions. The evolutionary character and impressive growth represented in the current prices of Solana (SOL), with an upward trend in its value, also gives it a taste of triumph in favor of the vast majority of Tokens that stand for thousands of projects that are built in favor of the Decentralized Finance (DeFi) sector.

After a brief visit to the network, consultation, brainstorming or comments among participants and connoisseurs of the crypto-asset market; we can demonstrate and even check, the way Solana (SOL) has been evolving, and the form of scalability that continues to reach its Token, with outstanding presence in thousands of exchanges, which allow it to be trend and maintain, through great efforts in a privileged position.

For Solana (SOL), it is an honor and a great satisfaction to be among the most important digital currencies in the world in such a short time, after its launch on the network. Solana (SOL) tokens represent a resource of extensive and timely financial and mercantile utility for business, trading, exchanges, staking and sales. The benefit or recognition does not come by itself, all this is due to the support that its software developers and technological support constantly provide to the platform, guaranteeing an effective, punctual, precise and efficient operation.

Let's be vigilant of the movement that crypto performs daily, since we have a Token that, in just one year has grown by almost 4,500%, high performance competitor against Ethereum (ETH) and the sixth currency with greater relevance. The outperformance that Solana (SOL) has given to Polkadot and Dogecoin, draws the attention of experts and recognized crypto connoisseurs around the world. Solana (SOL) continues its rapid growth as the sixth most important coin in terms of market capitalization value.

This is highlighted by the main web portals specialized in cryptocurrencies such as Investing and CoinMarketCap, which for the past November 3, published its value at 67,992,026.00 US dollars in the first hours of the day. For its users and future participants, it is worth considering that Solana (SOL) remains in frank growth movements. The currency continues to revalue as it continues to grow and reach levels that, in just one year, exceed 4,500%.

We could well assure that part of the success that revolves around Solana (SOL) is to be found in its recent gains inspired by the enthusiasm behind the initiatives reflected in Decentralized Finance (DeFi). So far in 2021, the Solana (SOL) token has skyrocketed in price by more than 8,870%, positioning it as one of the most powerful and impressive tokens on the market, in proportion.

Solana (SOL), a cryptocurrency, which all; is susceptible to high risk, but at the same time is a generator of great and significant rewards.

2

KEY TECHNOLOGIES THAT BRING SOLANA TO LIFE

The Proof of History, a cryptographic clock Solana (SOL), is the virtual currency that travels at full speed on the cryptographic highway, which leads to a safe encounter with Bitcoin (BTC), if the given conditions continue to favor its dizzying growth, but for the moment; it makes lights to Ethereum (ETH), whom it has right in front of it. And why this fast race? Solana (SOL) is considered, within the various Blockchains or Blockchain; as one of the fastest and most expeditious in the world.

We will see the importance of the time factor for a transaction and for the Blockchain itself, hence the complement of "Cryptographic Clock". In the meantime, let us keep in mind that there are many computational contributions to the cryptographic network that are endorsed day by day, and there will certainly be; and there are some. These are, then, certain updates that could feel as simple and exaggeratedly basic enough, but that, when applied to the Blockchain, generate a transforming and impacting stir; making itself felt as a resource or element of last generation, vital for the effectiveness in its operations.

For the existing Blockchains or Blockchain, it is impossible to generate consensus after the time that elapses through a given operation or transaction, this is because the nodes present in the network do not have or do not have the ability to establish contact with a common foundation to consolidate the variable of time. There is a focus of difficulty represented by the nodes in terms of achieving connectivity, since they will not be able to count on or rely on an equal provision of external time or time monitoring that will arrive via notification.

Let us illustrate a case in which a given user goes to a particular transaction through the Blockchain explorer; in addition to finding the operation, he will also have the information related to the time of that transaction, that is to say; he will be able to see the exact time in which the specific transaction was carried out, the precise instant in which the network node of the Blockchain explorer managed to register.

A cryptographic clock, can you imagine it?

A fully decentralized clock with applicability to the network in its entirety, capable of determining more than the time at which a particular transaction was performed and not precisely from the generic explorer of the Blockchain. Something like this, with such characteristics, precision and details, before Solana (SOL), had never existed. This monitoring, movement or check is what the platform in question baptized with the name of "Proof Of History" (PoH), an unprecedented model of Blockchain architecture.

Solana (SOL) stands out for having a unique tool to its credit, inherent to its own structure, a wonderful source of time as is the "Proof Of History" (PoH), a protocol that allows the network in its entirety, effective communication between all nodes. This novelty is so fast and effective that it travels through high-speed channels leaving only a flash of light in its wake, leaving on the bench all that was previously available in the crypto market prior to its appearance.

Bitcoin (BTC) is the main cryptographic reference in the world, which we have to recognize and not at all ignore. However, let's look at this interesting example:

The maximum number of transactions supported by the Bitcoin (BTC) digital network is 7 TPS, (7 Transactions Per Second) Solana (SOL) is one rung away from giving with Ethereum (ETH), innovative for the management of its Smarts Contracts (Smart Contracts). Ethereum (ETH), through its network, supports a maximum of 15 / 16 TPS, 15 to 16 (Transactions Per Second).

Solana (SOL), a recently created digital currency that grows intelligently with audacity, makes a great contribution to the crypto ecosystem, ranking among the first six best known virtual currencies and of greater value in the world, has the prestige of managing, supporting and contributing to the network a little more than 50,000 TPS, (Transactions Per Second); allowing the privilege of being able to compete with large centralized recognized providers such as the giant Amazon Web Services.

Given the magnitude of its structure, this allows it the power to soar and achieve a performance and profit at every moment of higher level. Of relative and proportional action, it is fascinating to see and verify how and to the extent that computers and computers are faster; much greater is the performance and speed potentially enjoyed by network transactions.

Among the Blockchains Blockchain, with the highest performance in the entire network, worldwide, we find Solana (SOL); a platform that has 200 nodes to its credit, structurally different from each other, which support a much more than 50,000 TPS, 50,000 (Transactions Per Second), after execution with GPU (Graphics Processing Unit). The magnitude of the timing arrangements are relevant, big challenges in all systems, but which Solana (SOL) handles tactically and effectively.

For timing purposes, we have the case of Bitcoin (BTC), which uses the Proof of Work (PoW) algorithm as a guide or decentralized time clock in favor of its operating software. For the same cases, we have on the other hand Solana (SOL), using its innovative "Proof Of History" (PoH) tool. Thanks to PoH, Solana (SOL) has the ability to devise its own log history capable of demonstrating with all the details, the specific moment in time that an event occurs.

All this occurs according to the action performed by the algorithm, whose verifiable function is characterized by a very high frequency. Its function, in order to achieve its objective, requires a sufficiently precise number of sequential steps and levels subject to evaluation.

In the "Proof Of History" (PoH), the operations or procedures subject to assessment or evaluation are assigned a unique Hash, computational power to process transactions and that by means of or through a count that can be verified publicly, guaranteeing and demonstrating its effectiveness.

What does a recount allow?

To give the exact data and information of when and at what moment a transaction or procedure was carried out, the instant when it occurred. Something like a stamp on the cryptographic time scale. In addition to this, it is important to know that inside each of the nodes there is a cryptographic clock in charge of timing the passage of time within the crypto ecosystem and when each event occurs or takes place, as well as its chronological order. All of this gives Solana (SOL) a truly high-level performance and robustness across the entire digital network.

The "Proof Of History" (PoH), is in essence a pre-consensus clock. Its algorithm opens the door to creating higher impact efficiency and a much more productive rate of performance from within the Solana (SOL) platform. In such a way that, by having a detail of historical movements of transactions, events and procedures, it gives the system the power to carry out a much simpler and easier follow-up, in addition to organizing all activity chronologically, as each and every one of the movements carried out has occurred.

Given the demand for platforms that meet the requirements, requests and needs of their users, there are many foundations, organizations and developers that make offers from their own platforms in favor of the cryptographic space and that are still on standby, the vast majority of these, if not all, after the launch of Ethereum (ETH), claiming to have found the resolution of conflicts in the disturbing dilemma due to the existing contradictions between them, with decentralization, security blockchain and scalability. Before the many projects that continue to design and plan strategies, in search of solutions and an effective medium- or long-term exit; Solana (SOL) appears, fulfilling and consolidating the network, making an activation of operations and transactions much more rewarding.

Although the Solana (SOL) Main Net is still in beta mode, its strength in speed and speed, together with the best rates per transaction, allow the Solana (SOL) network to become the ideal and preferred tool for applications in the Decentralized Finance (DeFi) sector. Solana (SOL) is already knocking on Ethereum's (ETH) door, and from its position it sees the light coming out of its windows, so long-term competition is imminent; it seems that Ethereum (ETH) already has a fully identified opponent.

And the fact is that, if we make comparisons and see the basics of their activity Ethereum (ETH) and Solana (SOL) in numbers, we find that, for one million transactions in Ethereum (ETH), 300,000.00 US dollars are paid, while for one million transactions in Solana (SOL), an average of 10.00 US dollars is paid; that is, 0.00001 USD for each transaction.

Sam Bankman-Fried is the Chief Executive Officer (CEO) and founder of FTX, a crypto exchange platform, is also the creator of Serum Exchange (DEX); one of the most popular Apps based entirely on Solana (SOL). To its credit and as a flagship resource, Serum

Exchange has an Order Book, not at all common for a DEX; strikingly low fees and execution of transactions in a millisecond.

Serum Exchange, is followed by Raydium; another crypto exchange platform also based on Solana (SOL), which has an architecture similar enough to Uniswap automated market making protocols, a protocol in Ethereum (ETH) for ERC-20 token exchange, designed to be used without platform or exchange fees.

Every transaction, procedure or event that arises in the Solana Blockchain (SOL), automatically produces a cryptographic function called Hash. It is a mathematical algorithm that modifies a block of data into a new fixed-length character string. This Hash is based on the SHA256 encryption algorithm.

The characteristic of this algorithm is that it is assigned an output that will be difficult to predict.

What does Solana (SOL) do?

It takes the output Hash of the transaction in question, which it will use as the input resource for the Hash that follows. The effect of this process is the input in strict transaction order towards the next output.

Through the continuous monitoring of this protocol, the aim is to create a long chain without any interruptions in the selected transactions. Thanks to this, it is possible to obtain a verifiable and sufficiently clear organization of all the transactions that will be added later to a block by a validator. By means of this "Step by Step", it will not be necessary at all to generate a TimeStamp or time stamp, a tiny piece of data that is stored in each block as a unique serial.

This is something that does occur in the cases of Bitcoin (BTC), Ethereum (ETH) and LiteCoin (LTC). Each and every Hash, will need a certain period of time to achieve completion. This time factor will also provide all validators with a simple, fast and easier verification of the elapsed time.

The Solana (SOL) "Proof Of History" (PoH), in comparison to the Bitcoin (BTC) and Ethereum (ETH) "Proof Of Work" (PoW) consensus, brings together an important set of differences. In the case of the latter two cryptocurrencies, it is worth noting that they proceed to group all their transactions in blocks, but without any kind of order or correlative.

In the case of "Proof Of Work" (PoW), miners simply report the inclusion of a TimeStamp, which consists only of the time and date on which a block has been generated or created, according to the Blockchain clock in particular. There is an aspect that is not only relevant but also delicate and very worrying, and that is that the TimeStamp varies according to and depending on the node. The most alarming thing is that this information could become irresponsibly non-existent or false. This fact obliges the nodes to perform a duly detailed re-verification of the TimeStamp and confirm that it is valid and indeed correct, timely and accurate, in order to ensure an optimal closure.

As long as the process or mechanism for organizing hashes is carried out and performed in strict order and correlativity, the group of validators will have less information to access for processing and verifying each and every block already generated or closed. It is advisable to use a version with the last state Hash for a transaction, since in this way the time dedicated to the validation, verification and confirmation of new blocks is reduced to a minimum expression and higher performance.

It could be said that the Solana (SOL) "Proof Of History" (PoH) is not expressly a consensus mechanism, but a tool or resource capable of seeking a solution with the objective of saving and reducing the time spent on confirming transactions.

In fact, Solana's (SOL) "Proof Of History" (PoH) is a complementary element in addition to the "Proof Of Stake" (PoS), in order to minimize the random selection of block validators. Similarly, Solana's (SOL) "Proof Of History" (PoH) makes it easier for nodes to validate the order of transactions in shorter periods of time. This will provide the network with express fluidity and much more speed in its processes, procedures and negotiations; more speed and speed mean less time to spend on each confirmation.

Solana's (SOL) "Proof Of History" (PoH) is a succession of calculations that may well provide an adequate means of cryptographic verification in the passage of time consumed between two transactions or events. "Proof Of History (PoH) uses a specific cryptographic function that is secure enough so that the output mechanism cannot be predicted from its input and must be executed in its entirety to generate the output from the input. The function is activated or processed in sequence from the same kernel, taking into consideration its previous output as its current input.

In a next step, the output could be validated and verified by external computational equipment that in parallel will proceed to check each sequential segment in a separate kernel. The data could carry with it, as we have already stated, a time stamp with precise, specific and timely information.

Well, with the arrival of Solana's (SOL) "Proof Of History" (PoH), a new history begins to be written in the existence of the cryptographic spectrum and a before and after in this fascinating ecosystem. Something like talking about Mars, our Red Planet, before and after Elon Musk.

It is already more than 10 years, a decade of life with which the crypto-verse, the digital mercantile and financial world together with the Blockchain. We are talking about an ecosystem that has seen the birth of thousands of cryptocurrencies and, in the same way, has seen them fade away. All of them offer or provide solutions to a new and innovative trend, however, it is not determined for sure which one is indeed the best, the most comprehensive or which one meets the expectations of the market, which one has the most secure consensus method, is the fastest or which one is the least expensive. All digital currencies that appear are welcomed, received and accepted with expectation.

They appear in the network with a set of excellent and wonderful technological resources of great advanced, surprising Apps and very interesting consensus protocols, among which we have "Proof of Work" (PoW), "Proof of Stake" (PoS), "Delegated Proof of Stake"

(DPoS) and many others that make up a long list of supports to a market that requires, consolidates and manages them constantly.

Today we have a new consensus protocol, which has aroused great interest and everyone likes it, it is a very attractive resource that we have been developing subtly. We are talking about Solana's (SOL) "Proof of History" (PoH), which, thanks to the optimal use of time, makes time lapses in transactions and much more profitable.

Merits must always be recognized. We have, for example, the cases of Bitcoin (BTC) and Ethereum (ETH), strong and sustainable cryptocurrencies in their respective positions within the cryptographic ranking, universally accepted and highly recognized for being the forerunners in the conceptions about the relevance generated by the application of Blockchain technology and, in addition, being flagship in the constitution of Smart Contracts, respectively.

Bitcoin (BTC) and Ethereum (ETH), are very well known, daily "receiving roses and applause", however, they are also the target of strong and great criticism given cases such as the lack of scalability and the high costs that represent the validation processes in the transactions in each of their corresponding Blockchain blockchains.

The cryptographic world, since its inception 11 years ago, does not rest; and is dedicated to seek and achieve the solution or find the resources to find the resolution to conflicts that, although manageable, deserve special attention. All developers around the world are certain that the most important thing is to overcome the difficulties generated by high costs and scalability, avoiding at all costs sacrificing or damaging the decentralization and security of the platforms.

Among the most recent acquisitions that the network has is the "Proof Of History" (PoH), created by Solana (SOL). Recall that it is a Blockchain consensus algorithm that complements the "Proof of Stake" (PoS) method, and that its premise is to speed up the consensus process, providing a channel that allows you to perform encryption of the time itself within the blockchain; allowing the nodes of the network the cryptographic verification at the right time and in the right order of how the transactions or events are occurring and developing, without eclipsing at all the trust and respect that the nodes have for the TimeStamps timestamps.

There are many benefits, tranquility and confidence that the implementation of this wonderful PoH consensus process around the entire cryptographic network produces to all validators and participants of the crypto ecosystem. One aspect that deserves to be recognized is the fact that validators are no longer forced or in need of having to communicate with each other to be aware or know what event has occurred in the network and in what circle of time or moment that could well be uncertain. The "Proof Of History" (PoH), guarantees the veracity of that moment, besides avoiding the achievement of conflicts produced in the "Proof of Work" (PoW) process.

The primary and clear objective of the "Proof of History" (PoH), created by Solana (SOL), a ratification procedure that makes clear a specific event in a certain space of time, which in turn is an innovative resource whose flourishing underlies the very technology of Solana (SOL), is dedicated to fulfilling the goal of "lightening the load of network nodes" within the processing blocks, at the instant of supplying a means of encoding time from and within the Blockchain or Solana Blockchain (SOL).

Generally, in the everyday environment of a Blockchain such as Bitcoin (BTC) and Ethereum (ETH), the process or passage of time is based on a sequential production and contiguous organization and order of blocks, this process tends to slow down excessively the various processes of verification and validation among others; especially the wait for the entire network to confirm the same transaction and then proceed to add the corresponding blockchain.

ABOUT THEIR OWN CONSENSUS PROTOCOL, **"Proof of History" (Proof Of History - PoH), the Solana (SOL) team once expressed, and we quote:**

. . .

"At Solana, we believe that Proof of History - PoH, provides the solution on the difficulty that is consensus over time in distributed systems. And we have created our own Blockchain around this solution. Some argue that the most essential feature of Bitcoin's Proof of Work - PoW algorithm is to function as a decentralized clock for the nodes that assemble the Blockchain."

WITH THIS STATEMENT, Solana (SOL) considers to be the Blockchain that has generated the resource capable of providing the solution to major conflicts; especially the very slow movements that overly affect the time in distributed systems diligent in the verification and validation of events in the network. However, the Solana (SOL) team admits that there are many users who consider the "Proof of Work" (PoW) protocol as the system that has the decentralized clock through which the Blockchain receives the nodes already assembled and organized chronologically.

In the meantime, other Blockchains are forced to have their validators maintain constant communication, and in this way gather information about what is happening in the network in the best approximate time; from Solana (SOL). A proprietary cryptographic clock encodes the passage of time using a simple function identified as the Sequential Hashing Verifiable Delay Function (VDF) or SAH-256.

"Proof Of History" (PoH), belonging to the Blockchain Solana (SOL), is a resource used to lighten the load on network nodes in block processing by providing a method of encoding time in the Blockchain. When referring to a regular blockchain, reaching consensus on the time spent to extract a block is essential, as is reaching consensus on the existence of

Therefore, the TimeStamps timestamp is important because it lets the network know that transactions took place in a particular sequence. Basically, Solana's (SOL) "Proof Of History" (PoH) allows you to create a historical record that shows that an event took place at a particular time.

So, how does the proof of history work?

In the case of "Proof of Work" (PoW), the successful block miner becomes the first to find the correct node (NAANS), short for number used only once, which represents an integer used as input for the current block's Hash rate calculation function, which needs a particular amount of computing power to run. But the "Proof Of History" (PoH) is based on a new cryptographic concept, known as Verifiable Delay Function (VDF).

It is possible to solve a Verifiable Delay Function (VDF) with a single CPU core using an exact set of sequential steps: suh, kwen and shl. Since parallel processing is not allowed, it is easy to determine exactly how long it took to apply those steps. Thus, the time step is definitely clear.

Since Proof Of History (PoH) basically solves the time challenge, the processing weight of the Blockchain blockchain, has changed, making it faster and lighter. Solana (SOL) is the blockchain that made this way of working popular. Solana (SOL) also uses Proof Of History (PoH) and a security protocol known as Tower Byzantine Fault Tolerance.

This allows participants to bet tokens and in this peculiar way vote on the validity of a Proof Of History (PoH) hash. If a bad actor votes for a fork that does not match the Proof Of History (PoH) records, he will be penalized. Solana (SOL) also relies on the Proof of Stake (PoS) to establish who can be a block validator.

Now, how fast does it all happen?

Since there is no dependence on local computer cryptographic clocks or local timeouts between state transitions beyond the verifiable delay function, the Verifiable Delay Function (VDF) will ensure that each block producer can prove that it has waited the necessary amount of time for the network to move forward.

The next producer needs to locally generate a part of the Verifiable Delay Function (VDF) up to the scheduled slot. This means that as soon as the nodes are received, the state transition can begin just as the message is received. This is because there is now a cryptographic proof and that the producer followed the protocol delays. In contrast, while Solana (SOL) confirms 25 blocks proposed by 25 different validators, other networks could only confirm 1. In many instances there are delays. The message may arrive out of order while the cost of network delays is slowly accommodated after the delivery of many packets. As soon as the "Proof Of History" (PoH) is reconstructed, the entire data structure makes sure that the appropriate delays found among all block producers are correct.

This means that the network is never delayed, and even with the variations caused by the block producers, it can still produce at ultrafast speeds. Therefore, "Proof Of History" (PoH), is the mechanism that enables network speeds never before seen in Blockchain technology. To all these, Proof Of History (PoH) allows users to create a historical record that functions as proof that an event occurred at a specific point in time, making the network more secure, faster and lighter.

The Blockchain universe does not stop growing, some blockchains are breaking away from the first generations and are also overcoming the scalability limitations of transaction speed and confirmation times. One of these new generation Blockchain is Solana (SOL), a crypto focused on the speed of its secure and censorship-resistant transactions.

Solana (SOL) is a Blockchain that boasts a novel transaction verification method to change the cryptocurrency market. Solana (SOL) is a third-generation platform that uses Proof of Stake (PoS) as its consensus protocol, however, it has added a unique way to determine the timing of a transaction called Proof Of History (PoH). Bitcoin (BTC) for example.

This groups; as mentioned above, its transactions into blocks with a single timestamp, in which each node has to validate these blocks in consensus with other nodes a process that entails a considerable waiting time until all nodes confirm a block in the entire cryptographic network. In contrast, Solana (SOL) transactions are encrypted and take the result of a transaction and use it as input for the next Hash by incorporating the order of transactions within the result of the Hash.

The process described above creates a long, unbroken chain of transactions with a Hash so that a clear and verifiable order of transactions that a validator adds to a block can be established without the need for a conventional timestamp. "Proof Of History" (PoH), is not itself a consensus mechanism, but is an enhancement of "Proof Of Stake" (PoS), which optimizes the transaction order confirmation time.

The confirmations in Solana (SOL), are defined by the time that elapses since the so-called random leader node marks the time of a new entry until the moment it recognizes a majority of votes in the Solana (SOL) record within the time it takes to send messages to all nodes which is proportional to the square of the number of nodes and this allows maintaining a historical record that accelerates its speed due to these technical characteristics.

Solana (SOL) has the ability to, in block times of approximately 400 milliseconds, a great advantage over the 10 minutes that a Bitcoin (BTC) transaction takes.

As it is a platform with a "Proof of Stake" (PoS) consensus mechanism, native token holders can only stake part of those tokens with validators that process transactions on the network. The validator who completes a transaction can share part of his reward with the holder who provided him with those Tokens, this reward mechanism incentivizes validators and delegates to always act in the interest of the network plus as with other cryptocurrencies, Tokens only serve to pay the transaction fees of the network and some of them are burned by the network itself as part of its deflation model.

Solana (SOL) allows developers to build Smart Contracts and create projects based on the technology. Much of the speed and growth potential of this Blockchain has driven the deployment of decentralized applications.

Why is Solana's Proof of History so important?

Solana (SOL), debuts on the crypto network officially in the month of March 2020, and in breakneck fashion begins an unstoppable ascent until it finds itself on the road to the pinnacle with a great walled wall guarded by the most powerful warriors of the crypto-verse, ready to take a gamble not to let themselves be run over, but also to fight to reach the top, which is under the power and control of Bitcoin (BTC), the largest and most valuable currency in the world.

Between one word and another, we said in previous excerpts in this and the previous chapter, that each virtual currency arrives on the network with some resource or differentiating element; an aspect that allows it to provide facilities or solutions to certain conflicts that perhaps some have offered and the community is still waiting to see them in action.

It is an ecosystem of very special and sufficiently varied "economic species" that nourish the network constantly and at every moment, a network that fluctuates in prices and capitalization according to the dynamics of each crypto, where a coin can change its position in the ranking in a matter of minutes.

An exemplary case of the above is Solana (SOL), which at the beginning of the first week of November 2021 was ranked as the sixth most powerful coin on the network, and in just three days it has climbed to number four! with a price of 242.09 US dollars and a market capitalization of over 72,800,000,000,000.00 US dollars, with Binance Coin (BNB) in third place in front of it with a price of 555.09 US dollars and a market capitalization of 92,740,189. 954.00 US dollars, Ethereum (ETH) in second place with a price of 4,536.63 US dollars and a market capitalization of 536,243,967,134.00 US dollars and Bitcoin (BTC) in first place with a sustainable price of 61,876.08 US dollars and a mighty market capitalization of 1,167,198,931,531,580.00 US dollars.

Undoubtedly, the cryptographic network and the fascinating world of virtual finance never cease to amaze us. Meanwhile, in Categories Solana (SOL) is up by 3.86%, Cardano (ADA) is down by 4.36%, along with Tether with a slight drop of 0.01%; but these last three, raising their percentage in Decentralized Finance (DeFi), as follows: (SOL) 22.58%, (ADA) 0.63% and (USDT) 0.03%.

WILL it be possible to interpret this interesting rise of Solana (SOL), thanks to its consensus protocols, especially everything that has to do with the "Proof of History" (PoH)?

I EXPRESS HERE A VERY extensive questioning, however, fortunately, it does not look far-fetched at all, because the great contribution provided by Solana (SOL), every day strengthens more and more the process of validations and verifications of events that affect and greater confidence in the system, providing additional benefits to a digital currency that, in the most modest program of developers, works for a faster, safer and more secure platform; works for a faster, safer and more reliable platform; that despite the vulnerability to which it could be exposed, activates maintenance processes and protection mechanisms for itself, its participants, users and future customers.

It is not enough to be the fastest and most fluid Blockchain in the network, it is also important to endorse to the network an operational resource and a consensus mechanism or protocol that will benefit the system; this is the great importance of the "Proof of History" (PoH), created by Solana (SOL) and allows a wide range of virtual and material benefits, from the network to the reward and satisfaction of the validators.

Time is implacable, the hands, or digits of the clock do not stop; for it does not exist, it is not known, nor does it know of reverse or "after a brief pause"; there is absolutely nothing to hide from the clock, nor anything to stop it. When it comes to time, there is or appears the clock, the expert in managing and controlling time, perhaps the only thing it does, but better than any other. With it and against it all, it is impossible for the cryptographic network to battle, it is subject to it. It is then when a prominent character, creator of Solana (SOL), designs, plans and develops a unique system that promises to consolidate the abstract aspect of the time factor and its veracity in favor of cryptographic platforms.

"Proof Of History" (PoH) is in addition to speed, effectiveness and reliability; correct and truthful use of time. It is to identify with precision and exact details, the precise moment in which an event or digital transaction occurs. It is the confidence to ensure that there is no way to provide an erroneous information, identification, data or reference that detracts from the correct procedure of a validator. The "Proof Of History" (PoH) is a resource or properly said, the consensus protocol will prevent that, in a bilateral communication between validators, it is altered.

Let us remember that, before PoH, other protocols would have been the means through which any transaction validation is submitted, which in multiple occasions was or is issued with alterations, cases of false data have been detected, given the need to establish contact from one validator to another, to be aware and know what has happened at a certain time with certain and specific operations in the crypto ecosystem.

Effective communication and, as we have already stated, the optimal use of time within any context, will make a big difference to the extent that each and every one of its participants, within the cryptographic dynamics, in the specific case at hand, are valued and respected.

Perhaps and at a certain moment, behind a cup of coffee or in front of a computer; Anatoly Yakovenko, creator and founder of Solana (SOL), saw the need for honesty, courage and respect in favor of those who trust their economic resources and deposit their dreams in a digital currency, surely and especially to those who support his Solana (SOL) currency, a public and customers that have allowed, even to take it today to the fourth place in the ranking as one of the most important virtual currencies in the world, and that we can well check according to the Time Line of publications in the CoinMarketCap portal.

The "Proof Of History" (PoH) of Solana (SOL) is considered as a breakthrough for the time factor that means a lot for the blockchain. In addition to that, Solana (SOL) is estimated to be the leading and number one blockchain on the web scale around the world. With all this and these distinguished valuations, we could well say that this still debutant currency has all the necessary technological architecture to be on par with the transactional capacity that today's internet possesses.

The main hidden innovation, active in the background and underlying the Solana (SOL) network, is precisely the "Proof Of History" (PoH). And the name of this protocol gives consensus, it is precisely and precisely what the platform suggests. A chronological correlative, a detailed and properly identified report, with a due order of each and every one of the historical movements that are executed and processed within the cryptographic network, in its daily, frequent and continuous operations and transactions. It is a matter of detailing the events given millisecond by millisecond.

The use of this protocol gives rise to a record that demonstrates and gives evidence of when the specific event occurred. A procedure supported by a reliable computational mechanism. At this level, it does not require external communication and the participation of third parties who need to make inquiries about what happened and who may provide erroneous data. Just by reading it and imagining it, one feels that a considerable amount of time has elapsed. With the "Proof Of History" (PoH), the issuance of the information is by means of immediate digital intelligence, practically at the same time as the transaction is carried out.

A very interesting fact to consider, and that should produce or generate an important level of confidence in the community, is that each Solana (SOL) validator keeps its own cryptographic clock active, encoded over time by means of a simple VDF SHA-256 sequential variable delay function, Sequential Hashing Verifiable Delay Function (VDF) SAH-256. A high-end differential plus that bears no relation to the current standardized fundamentals, sedimented in sequential block production, which will be affected, without any doubt; by the tedious confirmation waiting times in the entire network, which prevents moving forward with the immediately followed step.

"Proof Of History" (Proof Of History - PoH), symbolizes for the financial digital ecosystem, the primordial advance towards the crypto architecture in favor of the platforms in terms of speed and fit. It is to dignify the work that mainly fulfills Solana (SOL), along with the support and support to crypto platforms.

The operation of the "Proof Of History" (PoH), is written in a simple way, but it is to consider that it comes from an arduous process of demanding and complex mechanisms by its developers and its founder Yakovenko.

Let's imagine that we go in Slow Cam mode, to enter the Tic-Tac of Solana's cryptographic clock (SOL). The data infrastructure, interlinking the messages, there is a cryptographic proof in relative order, along with the time given in each message within the historical record. Thus, all local clocks pass to a hidden plane and out of the range or reach of the network in PoH; in this way and in an automatic gradual way, the times are gradually adjusted in unison and leveling those probable delays that could have suffered the network as it is linked and reassembled.

This is why Solana (SOL) has the ability to push the boundaries of time in confirmation events, allowing the network to offer a positive and encouraging experience, just like a centralized system without having to put decentralization or security on the wall.

As we can see, the "Proof Of History" (PoH), gives the network an affluent of integrity, authorizing the network validators to make their revisions and calculations from the General Ledger itself, so much so that a validator has the full power to determine whether a node can be considered active (valid) or inactive (invalid), as well as the confirmation that the network has exposed a necessary number of votes so that the ledger can be considered valid or active.

It is not necessary or required that a validator receives the messages issued at the exact moment, for that, the Ledger will be assigned in a programmed and eventual way to each validator, and as consequently the issuance and registration of messages is part of the Ledger feed, the "Proof Of History" (PoH) provides the cryptographic security and attention on the fair and reliable creation of each message.

This interesting feature facilitates the optimization of the network, by means of a varied series of parameters, especially in terms of Block Time, a key component in the basic fundamentals in terms of efficiency and speed. Apart from Block Time, the Proof Of History (PoH) allows Solana (SOL) to optimize on block expansion (log200 (n)), countable storage (PetaBytes) in the network and throughput (50k-80k TPS).

The duration or elapse of time within the cryptographic scheme for a block, beyond representing a net number of transactions per second, corresponds to a quantifiable unit that serves the function of dividing centralized systems from decentralized Blockchains. Let's see in numbers and playing with our imagination, some examples of cryptographic clocks, compared with the "Proof Of History" (PoH) of Solana (SOL):

- Tendermint: 3-second timeout window.
- Algorand: 5-second timeout window.
- Libra: Timeout window for approximately 10 seconds.

THE SOLANA TESTNET (SOL), which is sedimented in practically the entire network, has a 400-millisecond timeout window for a surprisingly fast block time. It is a true leader designed for 4 consecutive blocks.

While Libra manages to confirm one block, Solana (SOL) manages to confirm 25 blocks designated to 25 different validators. In the case of Visa, for the confirmation of a point-to-point event, 2.4 seconds are needed for a confirmation. Compared to the entire network, only Solana (SOL) achieves the highest speed. Bitcoin

(BTC), Ethereum (ETH), nor Libra achieve a confirmation response that competes with the "Proof Of History" (PoH).

At the moment there are only two ways for classical distributed systems to service cryptographic clocks. Each of the messages emitted in the validation, carries with it a TimeStamp or timestamp that comes from the sender, this timestamp arrives signed as a guarantee of its verification.

In view of this process, the nodes proceed to dispatch all long-dated messages. This computation process is based on the existing differentiation between the TimeStamp and the traditional local clock. Then, the next objective is that the transactions under their own individual condition have their local timeout period prior to their expiration.

Tendermint has the characteristic of having what is known as a pre-commitment state, which represents a timeout represented by one second. Whoever continues in the generation of the block has the possibility of postponing or delaying the next block, taking into consideration that all the nodes of the network will be forced to remain in stand-by also for one second, from the same moment that the event or state transaction begins, which precedes the validation to then proceed to consider the next proposal.

In none of the presented cases it is possible to give faith to the local clocks of a proposer, since each node takes its provisions generating a delay that prevents the advances in the consensus state servers, guaranteeing in this way that the proposer acts in the best and most transparent way possible. Although the delays produced are necessary for the security and guarantee of the network, they are interpreted as late blocking times.

The consensus protocol of Satoshi Nakamoto, creator and founder of Bitcoin (BTC), incorporated into the network a very different way of dealing or interacting with cryptographic clocks. In Bitcoin (BTC) there is a "difficulty setting" that somehow or other imposes on the network the obligation to create at least one scheduled block every 10 minutes on a regular basis. For Ethereum (ETH) it is considered that the complexity must be subject to produce at least one Block Time every 15 seconds.

What differentiates Bitcoin (BTC) from Ethereum (ETH) may well be calculated in number of collisions. The shorter the Block Time is, the higher the possibility that a pair of nodes can generate the same block at the same precise moment, and the 15 seconds of blocking would possibly represent the lower maximum time of speed with which any chain of the peculiar Nakamoto style would be able to generate a new block.

The Solana (SOL) platform has recently dedicated itself to joining forces with the aim of incorporating a new approach or a new direction in the network that will result in a globalized platform that never suffers delays or delays. The Solana Consensus Protocol (SOL) is neither tied to nor dependent on local or computer clocks, nor on local timeout lapses of state transactions, only somewhat endorsed by the verifiable state function, Sequential Hashing Verifiable Delay Function (VDF).

However, the VDF assumes that each of the block producers confirms that it has been waiting for a certain period of time and evidences that the network is in a perfect state of progress. On the other hand, for Tendermint, whoever is responsible for the production of the following blocks, must fulfill the responsibility of generating, in the same environment, a part of the Sequential Hashing Verifiable Delay Function (VDF).

All this means that the nodes with the responsibility of receiving are able to start the "status transaction", once the message is received, since it contains a cryptographic confirmation certifying that the producer complied with the protocols and followed the indications of the delays. For some reason or other, messages may be received late and disconnected, after a value adjusted according to the network delay, which would make regular leveling. When the "Proof Of History" (PoH) is restored, the entire crypto-data infrastructure would assume that the blocking times and delays affecting the group of validators and related parties are correct. What is really significant that is expected from this functionality is the simple fact of guaranteeing that the network is never delayed and that it is guaranteed the possibility of continuing its productivity, with the rhythm and speeds at full speed, well above the alterations that could be generated by the block producers themselves. The "Proof Of History" (PoH), is considered as an impressive and wonderful mechanism, capable of releasing speeds that, for the moment, no other cryptocurrency can offer.

SOLANA (SOL) IS A VERY complex project, so much so that even many experts in the field have difficulties in understanding how it works.

ON THE SUBJECT of Proof of History - PoH, it is a "Proof of Stake" Blockchain (Proof Of Stake - PoS), i.e. it has validators who are responsible for verifying transactions, compensated with rewards that are paid in its native currency called (SOL). Its payout value to validators is 73% and slightly lower for delegates, this at the time of writing this article.

Remember, Solana (SOL) is a Proof Of Stake (PoS) blockchain and its Proof Of History (PoH) technology is simply one of its many components. Thanks to its TimeStamp, validating nodes in the network can organize transaction logs without having to first wait for other validating nodes to check their logs. A TimeStamp adds an additional level of security and enables much faster validation, as Solana can process between 50,000 and 65,000 transactions per second, making it one of the fastest first-layer blockchains in existence today.

According to Anatoly Yakovenko, its creator the number of transactions per second would be much, much higher; up to 700 thousand transactions per second, were it not for hardware limitations; so as better components become available on the market, Solana (SOL) would benefit from this. Now what makes Solana (SOL)'s number of transactions per second so impressive is that it also applies to its Smarts Contracts smart contracts.

Typically, the number of transactions per second of other competitors, referring only to basic transactions such as sending tokens and not complex applications such as using smart contracts. This puts Solana (SOL) in the top of the fastest smart contract blockchains worldwide. Some even claim that it is the fastest blockchain of all and this represents very good news for decentralized application developers.

So far most projects have been using the Ingenuity blockchain, many, many decentralized finance projects and many tokens rely entirely on Solana (SOL), a platform that seeks to offer a faster and cheaper alternative. All this, taking into account that Solana (SOL) is a Proof Of Stake (PoS) Blockchain. For Solana (SOL), validator nodes are responsible for verifying transactions and generating new blocks.

Virtually anyone holding their native currency could only have one node; however, the selection process favors people with more Proof Of Stake (PoS) funds, i.e. the more money you have in Solana (SOL), the more likely you are to be chosen as a validator node.

Each new validator takes turns to be the leader that produces new blocks in Solana (SOL). Each turn has a duration of 4 blocks, which is equivalent to about 400 milliseconds, nodes that attempt to corrupt the network or do not behave properly are punished by losing part of the funds they have blocked. Another important aspect is that in Solana (SOL) the validators are put together in groups called Clusters, which perform specific tasks. For example, you can have a Solana (SOL) Cluster, which will be responsible for hosting a decentralized Exchange and another Cluster that will be in charge of maintaining a decentralized virtual world as a Land center.

"PROOF OF HISTORY" (PoH) makes it possible for validators to classify and verify transactions much simpler and faster than other blockchains.

. . .

SPEED, effectiveness, scalability, trust and authenticity; this is what Proof Of History (PoH) is all about; and on top of that the great support given to the network. Let's take into account that Solana (SOL) is a recent altcoin, of incipient creation that has among its characteristics a wide range of mechanisms, applications and short-cuts that Bitcoin (BTC), the strongest of all cryptocurrencies in the world, does not have so far.

Among the many differentiating aspects, we can mention the decentralized applications (DApps), Non-Fungible Tokens (NFT) among others; being these, some of the applications that are at the hand of its users and to which the public is allowed to access to make them, their important allies when negotiating and exchanging within the crypto ecosystem. A contribution of power that Solana (SOL) offers to the crypto spectrum and especially to its users.

Certainly, Ether; what is the Blockchain or Ethereum (ETH) Blockchain, performs these same functions and actions on the network. On the other hand, Solana (SOL), take for granted and guaranteed the statement that, product of the creation of its own Blockchain or Blockchain, has a software that simple to produce it and practical and friendly enough to use it, additional to that; the scalable condition that it possesses is much more effective and enjoys a speed, so far unmatched if we compare it with Ether.

The fact is that Solana (SOL) fulfills part of its operational functionality under the use of its consensus protocol known as "Proof Of History" (PoH), instead of "Proof Of Stake" (PoS) which is applicable by Ether 2. 0 or the very popular and quite prominent "Proof of Work" (PoW), handled by the world's number 1, Bitcoin (BTC) and which, by a certain point in its existence, came to be operated with full confidence by Ether.

Having computers and computers that have the ability to create blocks, which in turn can form chains, is a great advantage that only Solana (SOL) offers to the ecosystem, users and validators, in addition to giving a range of speed and expertise unique and exclusive to the same "Proof Of History" (PoH), a faculty that is unmatched and that gives a great advantage and recognition to Solana (SOL).

Let's make a small exercise that allows us to print an X Ray type shot to these three systems or cryptographic resources of importance and great advanced:

"Proof of Work" (Proof of Work - PoW) in the Bitcoin (BTC) scheme: here the nodes, represented by computers, computers or in essence, teams of miners, travel in a race against time to reach the goal and come up with the resolution of a cryptographic puzzle or mathematical conflict, and thus put on record that, through hard work, detailed analysis and disciplined execution of large amounts of work, a block can be created and added to the chain or Blockchain.

"Proof of Stake" (PoS) in the Ether scheme

In this protocol or system, the node is chosen or selected randomly and eventually, with all the tranquility, serenity and security towards who at that moment has the highest participation, which can be interpreted as not all participants generate energetic wear with the sole purpose of "winning the race" against time, many will seek a save that will always be necessary to take the next step. Optimal and effective communication between computer equipment is a must, remember that energy consumption is an issue of another level.

"Proof Of History (PoH) in the Solana (SOL) scheme

This timely consensus protocol, unique, important and time-saving aware of the crypto spectrum, does not replicate the main features of the above mentioned proofs; namely "Proof Of Work" (PoW) in the Bitcoin (BTC) scheme or "Proof Of Stake (PoS) in the Ether scheme.

Solana (SOL), in a very timely manner, relies on a set of time stamps, thus fulfilling a wonderful communicational purpose, and that is that all participants have first-hand information that tells them the precise time at which an event has occurred in the network. Strictly specific details, that is to say, everything that happens in the cryptographic universe, an integral crypto-verse in every sense of the expression.

The fact that computers maintain a high degree or level of connection and communication, translates or interprets into greater speed and express use of time: Speed! Solana (SOL) consolidates its foundations on a unique mix of mechanisms between the consensus "Proof of Stake" (PoS) and "Proof of History" (PoH). This, in addition to the robust software that constitutes it; allows it to give rise to or be the creator of a block in approximately 400 milliseconds, while Ethereum (ETH) does the same in 10 seconds; not to mention Bitcoin, which generates it in 10 minutes.

Before a series of inopportune events and operational problems with Solana (SOL) began to occur, the platform managed to carry out more than 400,000 transactions in a second, which served as a learning experience and allowed for important and relevant improvements from that point on.

In terms of production levels, let's take into consideration that prior to the appearance of Ethereum 2.0, the platform in its original configuration, had the capacity to perform 30 transactions per second; which was surprising and admirable, today it is no longer so, today it has the capacity to be at 100,000 transactions per second and impresses many, that Bitcoin (BTC) is maintained in only 7 transactions.

Solana (SOL) has an admirable lead, being today, a pioneer in speed; surpassing Visa by far, every time in reference to the production of transactions per second. Visa's speed is striking, when it has the quality of producing 24,000 transactions per second; which taken to Solana (SOL), makes us see that this altcoin is fast enough and has the ability to operate with much more than any other. Scalability requires a great ally, for its optimization; this ally is called: Speed. Only accessibility with speed and robustness, will allow a digital currency to become a circulating within the network as a currency of worldwide and globalized dynamics.

If we were to review a kind of resume or curriculum vitae, which would present Solana (SOL) in detail, we would find that this crypto would be fulfilling almost all the requirements for its entry into the cryptographic game, where it participates with great behavior; especially against the largest that remain unbeatable and immovable in the second and first place respectively, Yes, we are referring to Bitcoin (BTC) and Ethereum (ETH).

We could well affirm that here it would be likely to come up with the answer or with the unequivocal reason why the rise in the value of Solana (SOL) remains so much in blue numbers, it would be the clearing of the doubt that many of us still have.

In some previous fragment we exposed the condition that Solana (SOL) has to serve as support and financial backing in favor of users of all level and condition, to small and big traders alike. This is where Solana (SOL) has set its target which, due to its characteristic speed, was the center of attention for certain governmental and institutional organizations.

This interesting protocol is conceived with the firm intention of consolidating itself under a low cost structure, guaranteeing effective scalability and unique speed in its processing.

3

SOLANA AND ITS BEGINNINGS: HISTORY AND FOUNDATION

T he history, origin and subsequent founding of Solana, whose native token is the SOL, has its bases and conception, based on a very own intention that was based on how and in what way those events and situations that take place around a distributed cryptographic ecosystem could be identified, behind a platform orchestrated in scalable and integral Smart Contracts, with the full capacity to host all types of applications inherent to cryptocurrency with high levels of utility, backed by an environment of unwavering evolution and constituted by a valuable human capital of developers and validators applied with a sense of belonging and identification with Solana (SOL), its plans and projects.

Making a bit of history, and going back to what may have been the motive that inspired Anatoly Yakovenko to create a cryptocurrency with its own characteristics, inclined to make a difference, offering and implementing his particular proposals, which others still do not fulfill; it is mandatory to share a public experience that would open the doors to a project that in record time, managed to reach the top positions among the most important digital currencies in the world.

We have been told that, Yakovenko; after a meeting and sharing among some friends and acquaintances, managed to capture the attention of those who would later become his colleagues and co-founders of Solana (SOL), whom he managed to convince along with a small group of people, also known; who would be his first collaborators and subsequent users, to whom he talked about the idea that revolved in his mind to generate an interesting cryptographic attraction.

We are told and we have read that, perhaps this scene had its moment after a sports morning, after a day of underwater field hockey or quite probably, at the end of one of the activities that Anatoly is so passionate about; after surfing in Solana Beach, San Diego California, on the west coast of the United States; the favorite place and practice that filled him with adrenaline his visits to the beach and in which he shared countless days of sun, sea, sand, many waves and enough excitement to awaken and set afloat his creativity.

Only Anatoly Yakovenko knows the precise event and day in which he received the support, backing and that yes for an answer that became the first big step that would light the first flame and give the first ray of light to an initiative that would transform the lives of many, venture into the crypto network and support financial activity in different parts of the world, In addition to supporting a system and a virtual environment that continues to search for strategies that will allow it to satisfy a large number of operational needs on the network and even outside it, when it seeks to attract the attention of new followers, users, validators and miners.

Going back to Solana's (SOL) initial moment, most of us voted to believe that it all started at the beach; Solana Beach was always a favorite place for Yakovenko and his friend Greg Fitzgerald to have fun and escape. Both agreed to start with a thorough evaluation, back in the first quarter of 2018, specifically in the month of March, product of this and other considerations, was given the possibility of hiring a small, but very well formed and trained working group, a staff with knowledge and suitable faculties, many already with extensive and proven experience in the digital and computer world.

With some bank funds and a modest economic backing, the team started the construction and materialization of the project at a powerful speed, and since then there has been no pause that justifies to stop growing and going in search of a better and better structure and architecture. Hence, Solana (SOL) is called "a curious high-speed Blockchain project", with a great ambition and healthy determination to give rise to a blockchain of significant performance that should not and does not need to resort to fragmentation.

Once the first functions and typologies of the Solana (SOL) project were considered already consolidated and established in the blockchain, the work and development staff started launching applications for testing networks. The results and reactions were immediately surprising, the great importance and value represented by external validators challenged the developers; who almost immediately embraced a line of approach, guidance and pro-active monitoring that found in the well-known Cosmos ecosystem, the Blockchain internet; a source of inspiration to launch a series of "Networks of Incentivized Proof" (NoIP) competitions, which were called "Tour de SOL", a resource to decentralize the network by offering IT resources.

This launching of competences has been active since its initial moment, meeting face to face with a great number of attacks and suffering innumerable errors that saw their solution near the immediacy, that is to say; recovery almost at the moment of the events. Acting to provide a response and solvency with all brevity and guarantee, provides a unique confidence in the main network, which in practically three semesters has become an element with proven stability and proven security, allowing application system developers to be hosted and supported in the project.

Let's remember that Solana (SOL) has been designed as a Blockchain with a scheme of specialization in the creation of "Decentralized Applications" (Dapps) characterized by its high volume of traffic and utility. This is the reason why Solana Network has been built on a diverse set of innovations that attract the attention of even its own developers, allowing Solana (SOL) to remain, even at the end of 2021, one of the fastest in the world today, in the face of the many and countless novelties of other altcoins, platforms and structures within the cryptoverse.

And when talking about applications, validators, supports and networks; it is essential that every blockchain counts on the search for "Decentralized Applications" (Dapps) and the creation of facilitating projects for the various operations that the network deserves in order to support and satisfy all types of financial and mercantile activity. In this sense, the cryptographic community must recognize that Solana (SOL), on this and other common issues, has also focused on being a platform for solutions and contributions since its inception, offering value and benefits.

A wide range of programs and supports, among which Solana Accelerator and the Solana Foundation stand out, fulfill a brilliant task of constant backing and support in favor of application developers. These individuals strive to find effective platforms that allow the creation or generation of decentralized applications and the very important scalable applications.

A reference of great importance and relevance within the beginnings and origins of Solana (SOL) is represented by the public presentation of the "Proof of History" (PoW) whitepaper. A consensus protocol that attracts a lot of attention and is the other side of the coin. It is an interesting consensus protocol that has consolidated its basis of operation and applicability, in the monitored chronological sequence of each transaction or event that occurs on the blockchain.

It is inevitable, or at least difficult, to mention at any time, the flagship and transformative protocol that has meant "Proof of

History" (PoW) for Solana (SOL) since its inception, for the platform itself, as for the network; well we would dare to express and exaggerate perhaps with total responsibility that it would be likely enough that Anatoly Yakovenko had first thought of this resource to then conceive Solana (SOL) as such. And the fact is that its impact on the net is, without any doubt, overwhelming.

And it is that based on the idea that it was necessary to create or design a Blockchain with the ability to be able to give the accurate time count on the network, and after some structure have a way to synchronize all events with accuracy and security; Solana (SOL) arises, as a whole advanced platform. While active at Mesosphere, Yakovenko experimented with his brilliant idea of creating the algorithm, which he did. Subsequently, his stay at Dropbox served as a stimulus and concrete motivation to complete his ideal and take it to the public, presenting an attractive work with high expectations.

With all these many ideas and concerns in mind and the desire and interest to sediment novelties in the crypto network, Anatoly has the fervent desire to provide an expeditious way to reach a way to solve an important area of opportunity that to date, many cryptocurrencies and platforms offered but failed to meet, or at least put in place with perhaps unfinished aspects or with an achievement of failures and errors that would result even in the alteration of information, and especially in the one related to the time factor.

That is where Yakovenko focuses his interest and energy, to use the time within the network in a more realistic way; especially in validations, where a strong bottleneck in transactions was getting tighter and tighter every day; when it became evident that platforms such as Bitcoin (BTC) and Ethereum (ETH) presented reports with altered data and out of the real time mark, only with the intention of "fixing" the error or "solving", inappropriately an event in the network, which in any case needs to be based on data and references according and adjusted to the reality of time, especially for the validation and confirmation of transactions monitored by validators.

The team behind Solana (SOL) Let's start by mentioning that Solana (SOL) in its context and general constitution, is not a group as such, a staff or a traditional and standard work team of people who come to a work center in order to comply with a regulatory schedule and the instructions of a supervisor, in the best "9 to 5" style. Nor will we say that it is a society of friends brought together with a common factor, an idea or a philosophy of the same line of thought for all. When we look at the team behind Solana (SOL), the fourth best cryptocurrency in the world, which in just a few months has reached historic levels and positions compared to its competitors, traveling at the speed of light, we can only imagine the mega infrastructure that makes it up.

First of all, it is imperative or obligatory to mention nothing less and nothing less than its founder, CEO and creator of this great idea called Solana Labs, in honor of the beach and surf meeting place that Anatoly shared with his friends. Another figure of great importance, who has made great contributions to the creation of this wonderful cryptographic alternative, is Greg Fitzgerald, co-founder of Solana Labs and who teamed up with Anatoly, who contacted him and who once teamed up at Qualcomm. Together they gave their best to materialize the idea, the project; a protocol that today the world knows as Solana (SOL), at this moment, the fourth most important and outstanding cryptocurrency in the world.

Subsequently, and after the motivation and optimistic atmosphere that began to be perceived in Solana Labs, many colleagues were attracted by the idea and this alternative that they were sure would give much to talk about in a positive way. The Anatoly-Greg duo, together with inspired, confident and knowledgeable colleagues, with extensive proven and proven experience, managed to design, plan and develop a process that would become the Solana consensus protocol with its token or native currency SOL, this in March 2020, in the midst of a pandemic that forced humanity to be confined to their homes and paralyzed the world to the point of living on the basis of strict coverage of basic needs.

There are those who assure that this same confinement, the increase of general network activities and leading a practically digital and virtual life, could have been a catapult for this cryptographic project that was established with solidity and in search of an improvement in the use of time in the cryptoverse.

Today Solana, the now yes; Team Solana, is formed by: Anatoly Yakovenko (CEO), Greg Fitzgerald (Co-Founder & CTO), Raj Gokal (COO), Eric Williams (Data Science and Tokenomics), Hsin-Ju Chuang (Head of Gowth), Stephen Akridge (Principal Engineer), Mihael Vines (Principal Engineer), Rob Walker (Principal Engineer), Jeff Levy (Operations), Pankarj Garg (Senior Stuff Engineer), Jack May (Senior Stuff Engineer) and Tyera Eulberg (Senior Engineer); as the main front responsible for doing all the best for Solana (SOL) and how much is linked to this cryptocurrency. We invite you to learn a little more about each of them at:

WWW.ICOBENCH.COM/ICO/SOLANA/TEAM

NOT EVERYTHING we have seen up to this point represents Solana (SOL) in its totality or in its maximum expression; there is something else, in fact, very important for Solana Labs, and that is its main headquarters located in Europe, specifically in the city of Zug, Switzerland. It is the Solana Foundation. A non-profit organization, whose main objective is decentralization, ensuring the growth of the cryptocurrency together with all its structure and the integral security of the Solana network in its entirety, and which offers a delegation program through which all validators have the possibility of being part of this exclusive program of the Solana Foundation, for which they must meet a series of certain and specific requirements and capacity requirements.

Each and every one of the participants selected after their previous application, are from the beginning completely eligible, since the Solana Foundation does not tend to discriminate; what could happen is that the application is left for a future program. Both Solana Labs and the Solana Foundation are concerned and interested in having validators and talent in general trained and oriented around the network itself. Here the main idea is a solid part of the basic or specific objective, which is to receive, help and guide the group of validators and staff in general to ensure and help with the decentralization of the network.

From the Solana Foundation there are many projects and training plans offered to participants, users and validators among many others interested in growing and knowing the crypto dynamics at the pace of the times.

There is an interesting "Server Program", it is a program for the acquisition of high-end material resources at economic rates and very low cost, which offers a basic package to get started effectively and very well oriented in the network. Also behind Solana (SOL) are the well-known Stake Groups. These are groups of integral and active participation with which it is intended to find participatory solutions to those threats or failures that certain entities strive to spread as resistance to censorship, the development and evolution of "Decentralized Finance" (DeFi) and decentralization itself.

The Solana Foundation represents a structure of vitality and highly indispensable support for the entire crypto ecosystem, in particular for those who make mercantile, financial and commercial life in the network. Of course, it has its mentors and builders, who are consultants for the architecture and the entire Solana conglomerate. There is no doubt that the first head or first source of orientation, light and guidance will be found in its creator or "Father of the Creature", as an anonymous participant told Anatoly Yakovenko, in a conference room in Los Angeles (California USA), while the founder of Solana was just presenting a training program for validators and looked at his watch, which he laughingly called "My Proof Of History", showing the importance of time.

Behind Solana, there are not only its founders, developers, trainers, engineers, marketing staff or the entire professional structure of the brand; there are also its users, visitors to the network and those who make exchanges through its proposals and offers; they make up the most important and valuable neuralgic and promotional point of the whole chain, the public, who with their word of mouth, experiences and experiences of all kinds; they carry in their hands mobile devices that keep them up to date with the movements and variations in real time of the true reports of all crypto activity such as; buying, selling, exchanges, validations, etc. all the way to your favorite wallet. This and more we are going to find behind Solana Labs, Solana (SOL) and Solana Foundation; which in essence is one; the same home.

And, as if that were not enough, day by day new partners are added who choose Solana (SOL) as their support for multiple activities and become part of the community that is backstage or behind this consensus protocol that continues its increase in customers, users, price, capitalization and raises its position in the ranking of the best currencies in the world.

We will mention some partners that are looking for support and momentum in Solana (SOL):

- **Audius:** With a firm intention to achieve long-term scaling, chooses Solana.
- **Circle:** Partners with Solana with the intention of pushing USDC towards the Solana (SOL) Blockchain.
- **Wormhole:** Convinced that the most viable option is the decentralized economy.
- **Torus:** Offering full support to Solana and providing tools for building scalable core applications.
- **DFuse:** Joining forces with Solana, DFuse also offers itself as an option in high-impact conflict resolution on the Blockchain.

And so, a large number of brands do the same for their benefit, starting from a professional alliance with Solana and Solana Foundation (SOL), thanks to its credibility and demonstration of effective potentialities in favor of serving a huge community that has not yet received that punctual and immediate response that in network is required to move forward, on time and above all things, with security, confidence and guarantee.

Solana (SOL), conceived by an outstanding professional, expert in engineering and programming, young of this always surprising digital era, will not allow itself to remain in a position that instead of catapulting its project, simply stops it, eclipsing it, to the point that it may disappear with hundreds of crypto that at most saw only a flash of light to be launched, although many of them into the void.

If it is a matter of competition, it is strong, difficult, complex and with thousands of participants in the field. Appearing in the contest, 12 years after Bitcoin (BTC), the world's first currency, was launched, and only three semesters later being three places behind it, is an excellent incentive and reward; is an excellent incentive and reward for the effort, which deserves to be celebrated with more projects, more updates, more alliances and more contribution of solutions that day by day, fortify the network generating a more convincing level of attraction, but surely that lasts in the real time of what we call and that we already know as cryptographic clock and behind the scenes of Solana; which is not only the valuable human resource; but its wonderful technological advances.

The Solana Foundation is constantly pleased to announce that its growth is exponential, and that its doors are open to accommodate proposals that are fully formed or that deserve to be improved, hence its important content of educational programming for everyone in general.

Solana's Advantages and Challenges

When we are asked to list advantages of something or someone, we automatically think that we will also be asked for the disadvantages; something quite common. However, when we are asked to mention advantages and challenges, it is very attractive, since this condition immediately conveys an image of great strength, since we can immediately consider that we will develop the theme about who has the ability to face situations that will be overcome with total guarantee.

Solana (SOL) emerges and represents an advanced cryptographic alternative, of which there is no doubt; it appears in the network and in record time it joins a surprising advanced race that takes it to the first places of the best and most outstanding virtual currencies in the world. It offers, together with many other resources, which go hand in hand with the Solana Foundation, through its training and education programs, alliances and other solid and stable strategies; a resource that "transformed the time" of the crypto-verse, by taking it to a real count and with unique characteristics that only the "Proof of History" (PoH), has been able to achieve, leaving the falsification or emission of erroneous data in the validations.

Let's see some of the advantages of Solana (SOL) and how this somehow drives to invest in it and understand it as a safe, reliable and interesting cryptocurrency.

It is a cryptocurrency that maintains its price constantly in an upward trend: With less than two years in the market, Solana (SOL) has managed to increase its price unstoppably. To the shock or surprise of many, Solana (SOL) managed to travel from US$1.50 to US$212.00 in an astonishing period of time. A staggering increase of over 14,000%, but which then begins a gradual movement in reverse, on par with the rest of its digital assets; thus coming down to reach US$157.85, just at the time this document is being written.

Once Solana (SOL) joined the cryptographic system of "Non Fungible Tokens" (NFT) and "Decentralized Finance" (DeFi), its price, and therefore its market capitalization tended to increase; even exceeding 200%, and thus by mid 2021 Solana (SOL) manages to enter the ranking of the top 10 currencies in the world.

ITS PERFORMANCE in the network generates great confidence:

As a result of its consensus protocol, scalability, establishment of applications and price and market mobility, which keep Solana (SOL) among the first four best virtual currencies, it has gained the interest and trust of government agencies and private organizations, as well as small and medium-sized enterprises.

Solana (SOL) enjoys receiving important alliances in investments in the constant of its journeys, reaching a wide range and spectrum of clients. In addition, it is an interesting and valuable port of applications seeking accommodation in this Blockchain, given its great advantages of scalability and functionality.

It is the fastest platform in the cryptographic network: While after its most recent update, Ethereum (ETH) manages to reach the striking sum of 100,000 transactions per second, there is Bitcoin (BTC) on the other hand, whose platform still remains at the figure of only 7 transactions in one second. Making the comparison of Bitcoin (BTC) against Ethereum (ETH), we find a difference of 99,993 above in favor of Ethereum (ETH), but when we meet the amount of transactions that manages to process Solana (SOL) in 400,000 transactions in a second.

This is speed, but it is not just the speed with which transactions move; it is the guarantee of a neat, efficient and mishap-free operation. An aspect that no other cryptocurrency so far has managed to match or at least come close to.

Proof of History (Proof of History PoH): The chronological boom in terms of cryptographic clock is held by Solana (SOL). We refer to a tool or resource, a consensus protocol that benefits the entire network, without distinction. More precisely, it is a Blockchain algorithm that has been used to complement the previously known consensus method "Proof of Stake" (PoS), by means of which it is possible to accelerate the network after consensus processes by providing an instrument for measuring and encoding time more immediately and accurately in the blockchain, generating reliable information in favor of the network nodes that will have accurate timestamps and cryptographic verification or validation in the unequivocal time of the event or transaction.

The purpose that has and is sought in Solana (SOL) through the "Proof of History" (PoH), is in principle to improve scalability through this relevant protocol, as already mentioned, is activated in conjunction with the "Proof of Stake" (Proof of Stake). This interesting mechanism or "Proof of History" (Proof of History - PoH), fulfills the great responsibility of organizing and verifying transactions within the Blockchain.

Solana (SOL) has an ecosystem of close to 400 DApps Although the Solana (SOL) Blockchain is still in its initial beta phase, it has to its credit approximately 400 "Decentralized Applications" (DApps), all supported by this new and innovative Blockchain.

Given the high level of amplification that Solana (SOL) possesses, and the variety of power of its own ecosystem; which includes an "Automated Market Maker" (AMM); There are multiple decentralized exchanges, games, platforms for buying and selling "Non Fungible Tokens" (NFTs), platforms for "Decentralized Finance" (DeFi), investment funds; among hundreds of them, which makes Solana (SOL), its platform for development and growth.

Something of relevance is the amount of funds and economic resources that these "Decentralized Applications" (DApps) generate; thanks to their commercial development, they produce billions of US dollars on a constant basis. Solana (SOL), maintains a perennial willingness to make its technology, advanced and different way to be known and to act in the network and the cryptoverse in general.

And so, although it seems incredible, there are many advantages that characterize Solana (SOL), and being active in a beta version; its power is already felt, its best propaganda are the applications hosted on this Blockchain and its consensus protocol that makes an incomparable difference.

Solana (SOL), will continue to surprise you with the many opportunities that it makes available to all Internet users who have the option to improve their finances and even their virtual ones.

With what we have told you so far in this article, we will take as a basis what we consider should be taken into account by Solana (SOL), as a challenge or what it should face.

Among its main challenges is knowing how to handle the struggle within the cryptographic ecosystem and its experience in the virtual world as physical-material. To understand itself as that Blockchain of philosophical bases that commune with the common interest of millions of users that make life in the digital economic world and who have known Solana (SOL), have used it and have adopted it as their most comfortable and effective management resource for negotiations. The training of its human capital InHouse, as well as its customers and users must be a priority, an unavoidable premise. The Solana Foundation provides training, growth and development programs for its employees, general public, developers and validators. To sediment education in one or several areas is the best thing that can be done in favor of the communities; knowing how to challenge the lack of knowledge represents the best investment for humanity.

Another great challenge is to fight to sustain the veracity and trust so necessary for those who place confidence and security in one platform or another, in a sale, a purchase or an exchange; those who invest or acquire a good, with timely, accurate, precise and timely reports and information. The well-known "Proof of History" (PoH) may not be the cryptographic lifeline, but it has brought to the ecosystem a new way of reporting, validating and verifying everything that happens on the network. Thanks to the "Proof of History" (PoH), the data are all reliable and guaranteed.

When we as consumers look for a product that meets our needs, we expect to find something that looks like us and that represents and covers what we aspire to and what we are determined to invest in. Regardless of what we want to buy, what we need or what we require, the feeling is the same, a good product that represents an excellent price-quality ratio, durability and satisfaction, whether tangible or intangible.

Solana (SOL), has the quality of gathering a very important number of advantages and characteristics that are at the consumer's, user's and subscriber's hand. Being positioned as one of the best cryptocurrencies in the world, having a stable and advanced architecture, means for the network to be an option that is among the best decision to acquire Solana (SOL), a project that makes a bold and cautious move as it gets closer and closer to a strong Ethereum (ETH).

Let's not forget that virtually every digital currency we know of has offered dispute resolution, immediate response, speed in transaction, scalability, low fees and many other areas of opportunity. Solana

(SOL), in much less than two years arrived, introduced itself, started its engines and in an almost parallel way brought with it the solutions for years awaited and offered by other very good digital currencies and Blockchains of trajectory.

Solana (SOL), the Blockchain with consensus protocols, applications, programs and services at the height of the market and tailored to its members and users. Solana (SOL) per se, represents from its founder Anatoly Yakovenko, a great challenge and a great advantage.

4

INVESTING IN SOLANA

B efore investing, let's know where the money is going to go, so that we know for sure where the money will flow.

Solana (SOL) is the Blockchain consensus protocol that has been characterized by its scalability, which gives it the opportunity to create and generate "Decentralized Applications" (DApps), in addition to the important "Smart Contracts" (Smart Contracts). Solana (SOL) stands out for having the quality of achieving the permanence of an innumerable number of nodes without the risk of generating great difficulties and conflicts in the network.

We are talking about a high-level Blockchain without any risk parallelism that would prevent its normal development and development. Solana (SOL) and its power in speed and speed in the different events and transactions, is based on its best cryptographic contribution, the "Proof of History" (PoH), a mechanism with the functionality of allowing each and every one of the nodes to be matched more quickly and effectively, in addition to doing so with the guarantee of a 100% reliable Time Report. This protocol is not susceptible to time disturbances; therefore, it is more efficient than any known "Proof of Stake" (PoS).

The project founded by Anatoly Yakovenko, Greg Fitzgerald and Eric Williams, which is about to celebrate two years of activity, enjoys great recognition for being, at this moment, the fourth most important cryptocurrency in the global network. Just four years ago, in 2017, the young Russian-born Anatoly Yakovenko wrote the entire draft content that constitutes the Solana White Paper; it includes a detailed and very well-detailed analysis of what it is, how it is applied and the way the "Proof of History" (Proof of History - PoH) works. After a short period of time, Yakovenko and Fitzgerald, who was also part of the team working with Anatoly at Qualcomm, write the project's Blockchain in Rust, a computer programming language.

In this document, or in the composition of this written project; the Blockchain is endorsed with the "Proof of History" (PoH), as an internal cryptographic clock. Once all this initial composition of the consensus protocol and its respective blockchain is conformed in the White Paper, both colleagues and partners decide that it is time to publicize the proposal, launch it to the market and thus found a new cryptocurrency of recent creation. So February 2017 arrives and the Yakovenko - Fitzgerald duo, make public the official version of their project and their White Paper, along with the TestNet that accompanies this new digital proposal in favor of the crypto verse.

Solana Labs, whose company was initially called "Loom", was founded in 2018, deserving its name to the town of Solana Beach, located in San Diego (United States), and from its very moment of activation, was given the task of bringing together groups of developers from the most recognized and largest technologies in the world, such as; Dropbox, Apple, Microsoft, Qualcomm and Google.

Practically and almost immediately, Solana Labs caught the attention of a significant number of investors, who arranged their venture capital, managing to raise in five quarters, exactly from the month of April 2018 to the month of July 2019, a sum of 20 million US dollars, approximately about 17 million euros. All this through the closed sale of tokens. One year later, at the beginning of the third quarter of 2020, the testnet of the project was launched and made public. This testnet received the name of Tour de SOL, as it is publicly known.

Solana Labs continues its frank growth, then for the year 2020, punctually in the month of June, the Solana Foundation is created, a non-profit organization focused and centered on the development of training and education programs in favor of the community, sedimenting topics related to decentralized technologies and cryptographic ecosystems among a multiple variety of topics and academic programs. For the same year, Solana Labs, makes a donation of 167 SOL tokens to the Solana Foundation along with all its intellectual property rights.

Now, regarding the functioning of Solana (SOL), we emphasize that its structure has the capacity to synchronize the nodes in an effective and guaranteed way, in terms of security and high speed. Something that does not happen in other platforms, since the synchronization is done in large quantities, by means of transactions stored in blocks. In this format, time consumption is much higher, since the transaction or event can only be carried out once the block has been constituted.

An illustrative case can be seen in the "Proof of Work" (PoW), where a lot of time is consumed, since an event in which several miners are pending to extract the same block should be avoided.

For the "Proof of Stake" (PoS) consensus protocol, the "Proof of Work" (PoW) does not apply, since in this mechanism the Time-Stamps or timestamps are applied. This process is fundamental and basic in the process, because thanks to it, the validators will be able to have the necessary information that indicates the organization of the blocks created in the Blockchain. The timestamps or Time-Stamps of the transaction are placed by the Blockchain in each and every block, guided by the consensus protocol "Proof of Stake" (PoS).

We must take into consideration that the nodes of a cryptographic network do not behave or act in unison, nor under the same synchronization, since they will depend on an internet connection, where all of them will be activated at different speeds and with different computers. Motivated to this, Time Stamps will be traveling in the crypto spectrum, maintaining their properties for a maximum time of two hours. So, the Blockchain will be forced to increase the time it takes to generate a new block. This reaction scheme will ensure that the timestamps are the true and original ones. This scheme is more than timely, "Proof of Work" (PoW), currently Ethereum (ETH) takes a block time of 14 seconds.

For Solana this time is even much shorter, thanks to its consensus protocol called "Proof of History" (Proof of History - PoH). The nodes of the network that play a leading role proceed to seal each block that has been worked on, making use of a cryptographic check.

To go more to the heart of the platform and knowing its structure, just a few additional aspects, before starting to invest.

The platform runs on the Tower BFT consensus, a mechanism endorsed to the "Proof of Stake" (PoS) protocol, taking into account that for its synchronization it uses the "Proof of History" (PoH) consensus protocol SOL, Solana's native token, is used for staking, collection and receipt of payment for transactions and project management.

Solana (SOL) represents a comprehensive and interesting cryptocurrency, with the ability to host hundreds of applications, Stable-Coins, oracles, Wallets and projects such as "Decentralized Finance" (DeFi) and many more.

In addition to those mentioned, there are others that make Solana (SOL) an increasingly popular and accepted project for countless negotiations: Galactic Marketplace, a marketplace for "Non Fungible Tokens" (NFTs) based on Solana.

Wormhole, a connection resource that will make feasible the interaction of the Solana Blockchain (SOL) with the BSC network,

Terra and Ethereum (ETH) Degenerate Ape Academy DAA, a quite popular and widely used mechanism. It is the collection of 10,000 monkeys made into cartoons.

Currently Solana (SOL) is above 240.00 US dollars and remains in fourth place in the ranking of the world's leading coins, with interesting levels in market capitalization quite optimistic, according to the CoinMarketcap portal. The year 2021 has remained, since its inception, very much in favor of the SOL token, which has grown by more than a hundred of its initial value. For the month of August 2021 its performance was multiplied by 3, a month of November arrives with numbers all in favor of Solana (SOL), unquestionably; an opportune moment to invest conscientiously in this cryptocurrency.

Solana (SOL) represents a very important and attractive project. It is an alternative and a source of investment that promises excellent dividends and profitability according to the amount you want to convert, you will always be earning and Solana (SOL) does not cease nor stop growing, being useful for the network and developing in the integral and economic aspect. Solana (SOL) is promising.

The growth of Solana (SOL) is satisfactory, palpable and verifiable, we are talking about a project that stars in large negotiations and that goes from the simple to the complex in the opening to support and endorse the interests in favor of altcoins, projects related to Ethereum, "Decentralized Finance" (Decentralized Finance - DeFi) and others.

Observing the way Solana (SOL) evolves, behaves and is treated in the network, we are encouraged, to say that the network is in a transition age of great interest, it becomes adult and begins to understand what it does not need and could sustain technological relationships with. It is striking that Solana (SOL) rises and grows up to more than times, while we see a Bitcoin (BTC) that during a whole year has only reflected an evolution and growth of a maximum of 68%. Let's keep betting on Solana (SOL), and let there be no fear of allocating amounts to invest in it, a crypto of great power and with flight through the heights, like that of the eagle.

Where to buy Solana?

The purchase of cryptocurrencies has a large number of variants that will depend proportionally on the tool or resource through which we decide to carry out the operation, this is done through the Exchange of our preference, because according to the utility that we give it, it will cover our expectations and with total security; it will satisfy our needs in the guarantee of the negotiation and benefits that it brings us.

Through the different Exchanges or exchange platforms, we buy and sell, these exchange platforms are the resource that will allow us to give movements to our crypto-currencies, that is to say; thanks to them, the Exchanges, our digital money moves. The ideal is to know that we are using a secure platform, really encrypted, reliable and of total guarantee; we do not recommend to use the first one you find just for general search, investigate, review, get to know it, consult, verify its history, listen to opinions and finally; choose the one that will make your assets, a use according to your requirements. In a few words, try to find the Exchange that fits your size and measure.

Users, owners and new participants of the cryptographic network, will have the possibility of making commercial payment movements with their electronic money through a very wide range of alternatives, and not only the purchase and sale of crypto-currencies; also the payment of goods, traditional banking operations such as transfers, obtaining cash, shoes, goods, clothes, pleasures, trips, payment of cards and any usual operation; for this, both should have the tool that allows the transfer of crypto money from account A to account B. Nowadays, it is very common to see more and more businesses, establishments and companies trading with cryptocurrencies.

You should always be careful and negotiate with partners of an Exchange or verifiable and reliable customers, only then your digital business experience will enjoy true satisfaction. Remember that, although we talk about an encrypted financial system, we are not exempt from scams and deceptions; hackers know very well how, when, with what and the precise moment to captivate unwary or naive customers, very passionate and surprise them with fraudulent purchases and sales, especially when it comes to some trend. And for this, before continuing; we believe it is appropriate to talk about a recent case for the date of this publication and that perhaps you already know it. It is about the big scam with the "Squid Game". A series that became trendy and famous in record time, produced millions in economic gains, received donations, becomes more popular every day in the market, and is sold in all formats; that is, from replicas of the costumes, to the doll and the traditional song, which is part of the childhood growing up in Asian homes.

The cryptocurrency originated and inspired by the famous Squid Game, ended up being a millionaire scam that only benefited its skillful and criminal developers, who took advantage of the world-wide success of the series to design and launch a whole decentralized structure that made them millionaires, after orchestrating a very well thought out trap. Undoubtedly, there is nothing more effective than playing with emotions, persuading with what everyone likes, attracts and takes away a large active capital, with the ease of stealing a candy from a child. This scam was easy, simple, fast and gave its creators the calculated and estimated results; they did not need to swindle any more.

The fraudulent millionaire operation that generated the "Squid Game" token, caused a deceitful disbursement of more than 3,380,000,000,000.00 million US dollars. The old saying goes: "All that glitters is not gold".

For the purchase of cryptocurrencies, we suggest spending a few minutes to know a little about the five best Exchanges or Exchange Houses known and that we mention below:

- **Coinbase:** It is the best known and most popular Exchange House in the world and the number one in the West. Originally from the United States, it enjoys a very high level of crypto-active security.
- **Bitpanda:** One of the most recognized Exchanges in

Europe, based in Austria. Like Coinbase, its reputation for security is very high.

- **Cex.io:** It enjoys great privilege for being a native of England, where restrictions are strict and its prestige extends to the United States, where it has an important market. Its security level is very high.
- **Binance:** For years it has remained at the top of the best Exchanges in the world. It is originally from China, and its reference in security and trust is high.
- **Kraken:** Since its foundation, it maintains its standard as one of the most outstanding in the world. Originally from the United States, it enjoys a very high level of crypto-active security.

ACCORDING TO STATISTICS, we are shown that the most popular and most used Exchange in the world is Coinbase, which is listed first in our previous list. However, and most probably due to a trading cost issue, Binance has a great power and presence in the market. While the trading cost of Coinbase is 0.50%, Binance is at 0.1% Binance is the exchange with more users in the world, and through it you can buy, but also sell Solana (SOL). The first thing you should do is to register and create your own account on its platform and through your Binance profile, start enjoying the world of cryptocurrency transactions. You will be able to manage your account from your mobile or your computer, and you will have the facility to make deposits whenever you need to.

To buy Solana (SOL), which is our particular case, we are not obliged to buy exclusively through Binance, Exchange that we are not sponsoring either; surely you have your own Exchange account with which you already operate, and surely in it you can buy and sell Solana (SOL), cryptocurrency that by the way is rumbling the bases of Binance (BNB) in the ranking of the best coins in the world that at this precise moment are in:

- Position No. 3: Binance (BNB) / Price: 635.46 USD.
- Rank No. 4: Solana (SOL) / Price: 244.24 USD

INFORMATION BASED ON COINMARKETCAP.COM SOURCE, **dated November 8, 2021.**

THE PROCESS TO buy Solana (SOL) is really quite easy, once you have completed the first step and you already have your Exchange account, what you have to do is to determine under which modality you will use to obtain the Solana (SOL) tokens you want or need.

Binance, for example, will offer a list of StablesCoins or stable digital tokens in fiat currency in order to maintain the value and stability of the exchange rate to be applied according to the currency through which you will obtain Solana (SOL).

Through a bank transfer, made with your application on the Binance platform, you will send your money to the account of this provider, holders of the Token, then, you will have the StablesCoins negotiated, with which you will make the purchase of Solana (SOL) directly on the Exchange.

You can also buy Solana (SOL) with your credit or debit card, performing the same steps, with the supply of your data on the card to be used. For this and other cases, Binance takes you step by step. A valuable aspect for the purchase of Solana (SOL), through Binance by credit or debit card, is the excellent and varied alternatives that the Exchange offers for the purchase of Solana (SOL) for Visa and/or Mastercard users.

In addition to the purchase of Solana (SOL), Binance also offers to the market in general and all its users, the admission and realization of deposits with more than 150 virtual currencies, among which there are some that can be exchanged for Solana (SOL), enjoying the most attractive and competitive rates for commissions seen in the market. This way of trading with Solana (SOL) is effective, interesting; which, during the first week of November 2021, has been very active.

The possibility to buy, sell, make deposits and trade with Solana (SOL) at any time, day and place you want is a complete reality. Binance offers its platform to be used, besides from a computer, through your cell phone device. You only need to download the Binance trading application via Google Play or App Store and you will have a useful and really necessary resource for those who move in today's world that revolves around the use of cryptocurrencies or the cryptographic system in all its splendor.

The purchase of Solana (SOL) is interesting, and a lot when we see that its value, although with slight drops; remains at important levels. Even the initiation procedure is quite simple and really practical. The registration in an Exchange does not result in the delivery of large and annoying requirements, it is just as if you were opening an email account or a new social network. An Exchange account or profile is kept secure, only you know and manage your username and password, as well as the resources and shortcuts to recover from possible hacker attacks or actions of third parties who try to enter and violate your account.

The funds to and from the Binance platform with your account are bilateral, and the exchange negotiations that are carried out in the Exchange ecosystem are protected and encrypted, only the participants of the transaction will be the ones who handle all the information of amounts, data and other operational references to which they have access.

Being immersed in the world of cryptocurrencies or being part of this financial ecosystem, every day is becoming more frequent, less and less fiat money we are handling, we constantly notice that coins and traditional banknotes are more absent; we are going less to the bank. Electronic transactions are the order of the day and purchases with and from electronic money are more common.

Remember to download the Exchange of your preference and

start funding your economic resources with Solana (SOL) and in addition to your usual bank account, start using your favorite wallet, this way you will be able to manage in the market with advanced elements, resources and structure.

Wallets that support the Solana (SOL) token Solana (SOL), is a platform that we have seen evolve modestly and forcefully in a very satisfactory way, and in its recent launch it has grown to a new level and Surprise! mode, because it has left many of us thoughtful and restless in terms of price, capitalization and the possibility of acquiring it, having Solana (SOL) in our virtual wallet or wallet.

Well, if you have ever thought of venturing into the world of cryptocurrencies and becoming a Solana (SOL) holder, there is no doubt that the time has come and you will see it reinforced in this easy, pleasant and enjoyable reading. We are going to share with you some interesting lines, in which you will find what we consider to be the best wallets for virtual currencies, and in a very special case, for Solana (SOL). We will see here the main possibilities currently available, together with the most attractive options.

Since its launch, last March 2020, Solana (SOL) has been at pains to make itself known as a next-generation Blockchain, offering its architecture as a solid foundation for the creation and firm establishment of innovative and world-class "Decentralized Applications" (DApps). These are important and weighty enough aspects that are among the main objectives of Solana (SOL) and on which its creators, staff and team of developers are working hard.

Solana (SOL) is based on the Proof of Stake (PoS) consensus protocol, a third generation mechanism. This consensus, in turn, is based on a procedure of high levels of trust and extreme security, sedimented in its "Proof of History" (PoH) protocol, which provides unprecedented levels of trust that at the time many cryptocurrencies claimed to install, but Solana (SOL) appeared with this card up its sleeve at the disposal of the virtual cryptographic network.

Solana (SOL) was devised and conceived from a blank sheet of paper, it is a totally unprecedented creation with its own DNA, which seeks true scalability. Its developers are seeking to demonstrate that the mixture of so many algorithms in the same Blockchain, will certainly cause great conflicts instead of improvements and greater operational potential, this can be translated into continuous network saturation.

The mentor and main ringleader of all this cryptographic structure is still its creator, Anatoly Yakovenko who started with Solana Labs for the year 2017, and who on behalf of Solana (SOL), designed this innovative consensus protocol called "Proof of History" (Proof of History - PoH), which must have and count on the ability to withstand hundreds and thousands of transactions per second at all times, as I have been demonstrating it until today.

Now, having said all the above, let's see and define what a wallet or wallet is, how useful it is and what is its presence or participation in the network.

THE TERM WALLET is an English word, which, literally translated into Spanish, means "wallet" and in turn comes to be the qualifier that is given to the digital resource that functions as a virtual support in which are stored and managed the login credentials to the cryptographic system and thus, from there; give use to the digital money which is available at a given time. It is very important to be clear that a wallet does not store cryptocurrencies, they are accumulated or kept in the relevant Blockchain or for use by the participant. In the wallets, you will be able to consult and verify the balance you have and you will be able to manage and use through an Exchange that allows you to buy, sell or exchange.

For a user or crypto-enthusiast to have the possibility of storing his own cryptocurrencies in particular, it will be necessary to have a wallet. This wallet or wallet has two characteristics, it can be used as software or it could also be a physical wallet. All this varies according to the person's needs and the type of wallet he/she believes convenient to use according to his/her needs, requirements and the level of security he/she wants to give to his/her funds.

In theory, a wallet is very useful if we want to have a recovery device and a private access key. From this private key, it is possible to generate a public key that will support our addresses and transactions.

The wallets allow the user to have the necessary access to his account statement or balance, to which he will be able to enter through his private key, as well as to carry out transactions with the currencies he owns. In general, all wallets give the user the possibility to receive and send digital currencies with a splendid and total ease with a margin of conflicts practically null. Other wallets may offer more and different functions. An example of this is the case of the Ethereum (ETH) Blockchain, in which it is approved to exchange Ether into Tokens or the opposite, with the well-known Wallets Lighthing Network in Bitcoin (BTC) or Metamaks, a wallet for cryptocurrencies.

Coin98

Easy and simple to use with somewhat limited apps. Today the App is only available for iOS and Android. Sends and receives SOL tokens without inconvenience.

Exodus

Allows receiving, sending and exchanging cryptocurrencies easily and friendly. Currently available for iOS, Android and Windows. It provides access to balance inquiries worldwide. Exodus has graphical charts and a comprehensive exchange system.

It offers 24-hour technical support.

Trust Wallet

It is an exclusive wallet for iOS and Android in which cryptocurrencies from the Solana Blockchain (SOL) can be stored. Its security factor is subject to access by third parties. Its developers suggest creating a private access code.

ZELCORE

Receives and sends all the tokens established in the Solana Blockchain (SOL), it is a multi-currency wallet. Zelcore accounts have three independent addresses. It is possible to connect, transact and store different dApps. Its developers are working to incorporate a DEX to expand capabilities.

Currently available for Windows, iOS and Android.

Web Wallet for Solana (SOL)

Next, we will learn about some wallets available for Solana (SOL), available on the web and reachable from the browser of our preference. These wallets offer us the opportunity to access decentralized Exchange easily and in a very simple way.

Phantom

Represents the branch of a decentralized browser, which grants access to Solana funds in a secure and simple way. It allows storing, exchanging, receiving and sending SOL among the other token types.

This wallet provides support for Non Fungible Tokens (NFT) and Ledger's HardWareWallet (HWW).

It is available for Edge, Brave, FireFox and Chrome.

SOLFLARE

This is a non-custodial developed exclusively by the community for Solana (SOL). SolFlare supports the creation and management of share accounts. It can receive and send tokens from the Solana (SOL) Blockchain.

Available on Brave, Edge and Chrome.

BITKEEP

Wallet that allows its users to receive and send SOL tokens from the Solana Blockchain (SOL). This wallet is compatible with Solana's (SOL) Decentralized Applications (Apps) without mishaps.

This wallet is available in most browsers.

SOLLET

Like Phantom and SolFare, this is a non-custodial wallet developed by the Project Serum team. It is currently in beta and is easy, simple and convenient enough to use.

MathWallet

It is a Multi - Wallet with the ability to support a wide variety of cryptocurrencies. This wallet allows receiving and sending Solana (SOL) cryptocurrencies. It is available in Web Version and also by browser extension.

Its availability for iOS and Android and iOS is not yet enabled by Solana (SOL) digital currency.

Hardware Wallets for Solana

For holders of large amounts of Solana (SOL), there is a modality through which they can access technological resources that will allow them to safeguard their funds and assets in a highly secure manner.

If what you are looking for is to avoid at all costs a possible attack or theft of credentials to access your cryptocurrencies, the most advisable is to have a Hardware Wallet.

Ledger Nano X / Ledger Nano S

To date we only have the information that the only hardware wallets that support the Solana (SOL) cryptocurrency are the Ledger Nano X and Ledger Nano S.

Both wallets are part of the most known Cold Wallets currently on the market, especially for their high degree and level of security. On the other hand, the Ledger Nano X wallet has encryption chips and features breach detection and anti-malware, it also has integrated the BOLOS operating system, which supports the installation of independent Apps, without having to interconnect any type of stored information.

Online wallet for Solana

These are those wallets that are offered by centralized Exchanges. Generally speaking, it is not advisable to download and use this type of wallets, and the reason is that the private keys will not be in the hands of the owner of the cryptocurrencies. As you can imagine, the cryptocurrencies you own are 100% vulnerable to crime and could be stolen by third parties as well as being blocked by the Exchange itself.

Recently the Chinese Exchange, Binance froze the movements to accounts of the European SEPA payment network for reasons that so far has not been disclosed and has not specified. Although it is clear that our assets can be withdrawn through other methods, here and with this situation it is totally evident that the risk of storing cryptocurrencies in centralized Exchanges, will represent a risk at all times both for those who store, as we have said, and for those who receive and/or send.

5

SOLANA TO THE MOON

S tarting in 2017, Solana (SOL) began to take its first steps, perhaps much earlier; perhaps in Yakovenko's subjective conception. To date we can confirm that this novel cryptocurrency already has to its credit an interesting and great journey with which, fulfilled a series of commitments, facing imposing challenges in a commercial and financial ecosystem that year after year has begun to consolidate thanks to the everyday emerging virtual currencies, Blockchains, applications and others that seek a space in the network, presenting itself as a new economic, mercantile and financial alternative of advanced.

We have had the opportunity to see the birth of many cryptocurrencies, but we have also regretted how others fade away and are definitively absent from the network. We have had the joy of having the support, backing, security, trust, loyalty and strength with cryptocurrencies that today continue to figure in the digital ranking; and we have also had the painful experience of witnessing scams and big frauds by tokens and other fleeting currencies, which disappear with millions of stolen monetary units or simply as a result of scams.

In this ecosystem, we regret the bad moments and unpleasant experiences, but we are also inspired and enjoy those positive experiences, which have generated great fruits and have benefited millions of people around the world, after the negotiation, exchange, purchase, sale, commercialization and other positive activities that are those that, in essence, in favor and thanks to the network, are more. That is to say, there are more good experiences than bad ones, and it is there; thanks to them that the whole cryptographic spectrum remains active, productive and attentive; ready to make itself a resource for socio-cultural and economic welfare. Offering and guaranteeing stability, a way to attract more and new investments.

There are currently more than 1,600 cryptocurrencies, all distributed through various platforms dedicated to their hosting, from the most specialized to the most modest. All of them have clear objectives in seeking to satisfy the needs of the market and its users, in addition to providing security and guarantee in transactions and different events on the network.

And it is precisely because they are decentralized markets, without dependence, supervision or management by traditional financial institutions, banks or government entities; there is a certain level of uncertainty for many or an important level of freedom to manage resources with certain, determined and very particular characteristics. Each cryptocurrency is a different philosophy, each cryptocurrency carries its own DNA, each cryptocurrency is unique; perhaps we could come to consider or believe that they all do the same thing, fulfill the same function, but for "something" they have different values.

Maybe for someone talking about Bitcoin (BTC) and Solana

(SOL) is "exactly the same", and any name of any cryptocurrency will sound like just "currency". And if we compare the crypto spectrum with a big orchestra, some interesting questions will come to mind: Why if 20 violinists are playing only 5, or "When the season started, there were 120 musicians, why are there only 40 musicians", or "When the season started, there were 120 musicians, why are there only 40 musicians?

In some common conversation among friends or if we take the press and in both cases the central topic is cryptocurrencies, these will be the names on the table: Bitcoin (BTC), Ethereum (ETH), Dogecoin (DOGE), Cardano (ADA), Solana (SOL); the same as always! Position earned thanks to their steadfast persistence.

And the fact is that many do not survive, do not exceed their own expectations or the market itself, after its energetic and changing dynamics, forces them to make changes or simply give way.

But something that influences and influences in an overly decisive way is the price represented by a cryptocurrency and its market capitalization.

In the traditional economic format, that which we knew before modern cryptography and which is governed by the guidelines of the central banks of governments, prices are set by the State itself, which determines a specific and unique legal tender currency, backed by its gold reserves. In this sense, the use and value given to and received by this national money will be established by the financial entity dictated by the government. The institution determines, signs and publishes.

The pricing of a cryptocurrency is on a clear and well-defined opposite line. The price and capitalization of a cryptocurrency is based and consolidated on the trust it receives from its users, consumers and participants; however, the value of each cryptocurrency is determined by the supply and demand of its tokens. This is a very important reference if we make a comparison between digital currency and traditional currency. Both financial systems are vastly different.

For a virtual currency, its value or price will never depend on the behavior of a specific national economy; it, the cryptocurrency will obey its behavior, according to the supply and demand of the token. The fact that cryptocurrencies are of cryptographic origin, dependent on a Blockchain, prevents them from being controlled. They will not depend on a reserve that backs them, as do the national and central banking entities of the countries that are governed by the well-known "Trust System", in which it is necessary to control the movement of cash circulating in order for their economies to perform; thanks to this dynamic of economic control, economic crises occur, as is the case of what is happening in Venezuela.

Cryptocurrencies are also vulnerable to financial conflicts, in them it will be easier for a situation of decline to occur; precisely because they have a fixed income. The fall of its price due to inflationary effects is quite improbable. The value of a digital currency is based on easily verifiable particularities:

Speed of change in the market, increase of users, trading volume, among others.

In essence, what makes the price of a cryptocurrency go up or down can be found in two unique and specific examples:

- **Situation A:** In case the transaction is carried out by two people or individuals, the price given to the cryptocurrency, will definitely be the one that both agree and decide to use to close the negotiation.
- **Situation B:** In the event that the transaction is carried out through a digital platform or an Exchange, the fixing of the price for the negotiation will be subject to the crossing result in the two transactions agreed upon by the participants: Buyer / Seller.

HOWEVER, if we pay attention to the changes that the network undergoes, to its dynamics, to the volatility and the different trends, movements and ideas, new inventions, the analysis will be extended. Motivated by the constant turmoil in the market prices, Solana (SOL) has aroused great interest in different organizations, companies and investors.

Lately, Solana (SOL) has not ceased to worry the cryptoverse, and one of the effects of special attention has been caused by its own goodness of its structure, its position in the ranking and the relationship between price, value and capitalization. There are many factors to consider, evaluate and assess around Solana (SOL), highlighting the projection of its price and consider the possibility of becoming a holder of this cryptocurrency to include it in our investment wallet.

If we travel a bit in time, and stop on Tuesday, July 21, 2020, we are going to find that this was the 1st day of trading recorded by Solana (SOL). For its debut, Solana (SOL) opened on the web with a price of 0.8729 US cents and closed at 0.9772 US cents. Such was the first day for the debutant.

On the other hand, and at the time this article is written, Sunday, November 7, 2021; we have that Solana (SOL) opened on the network with a price of 258.78 US dollars and closed at 249.82 US dollars.

The evolution of its price, in this chronological frame, with its respective intermediate fluctuations has registered an increase of 248.94 US dollars; an amazing 285,200% very well deserved. Now, and after a year and a half we ask ourselves:

Should you buy and invest in Solana (SOL)?

In short, yes, for the present moments and seeing only two historical extracts of this cryptocurrency, we can interpret the gradual and safe price evolution that Solana (SOL) has experienced, and for which it meets all the necessary qualities to be eligible as a digital currency, worthy of investment.

Solana (SOL) is a fabulous choice to decide to invest in it, we cannot deny under any circumstances that its permanence and movement in the network has been very effective, experiencing in more than a year very good numbers and a position of stable levels in the ranking of the best coins, according to CoinMarketCap.com. Gathering so many and all these positive qualities that Solana (SOL) possesses, evaluating its behavior, understanding this cryptocurrency according to its contributions to the network and convinced that it itself is showing us what it is and what it has to give; we cannot fall into a dilemma "looking for the fifth leg to the cat", when the table is already served. Solana (SOL) has everything to gain and become the best prepared cryptocurrency for a wonderful future.

With the trust placed in Solana (SOL), giving support to its platform, strengthening the token, multiplying the use of its resources and punctuating, besides spreading the positive, optimistic, enthusiastic and motivational messages towards this crypto; we would be contributing to it reaching an increase perhaps exceeding 100% of its value. At all times it is imperative to be very clear about the destination we would give to the capital we allocate to make an investment, here an exhortation not to anticipate the facts, but to consider the option to study, try to understand the cycle and act for when you consider it is the right time; the here and now of Solana (SOL).

An appropriate form of preparation for a future investment is observation and inquiry, read the press and try to understand the behavior of the object product of my future investment, who are its investors, what is its level in the market, try as much as possible to know and become familiar with the platform, to know what amount of money can be "put at risk" and any other detail that allows the interested party to know as well as possible the land that will begin to cultivate and to which the economic resources, obtained after his own effort, will be destined.

All of the above can be taken or considered as part of or as a guide for orientation towards conscious investment. Very basic, simple, practical and easy to perform steps. Many times we get carried away by passion, be careful here! A cryptocurrency can suddenly be in a position and a price tempting enough to invest immediately, maybe it is a cryptocurrency of insurmountable trend and fame that gave you the time to pass the filter of reason, and suddenly a fraudulent phenomenon occurs as in the case of the digital currency of "The Squid Game", which appeared on the network, bid, captivated, collected and scammed. A lot of fame, showbiz and fun and passion; why didn't they stop to think a little, see their behavior, heed the warning signs?

Will Solana's (SOL) value continue to rise?

It is like everything else, a matter of time. To give an immediate affirmative or negative answer to this important question, could be somewhat irresponsible, more if we can say that based on its stable positions and its impetuous increase with sufficiently slight drops, with really short peaks, are telling us that at least, and in the short term; there is a quite clear tendency to stability both in its price and capitalization.

If we can express, that, from now on, Solana (SOL) will surely be much more willing to defend its level, strive to continue making a difference, already remarkable and seek the means to continue contributing to the network and open and more its doors to the arrival of new Apps that choose its platform and its Blockchain as operational sustenance. It all adds up and with so many pros in its favor, we dare to close this paragraph, removing the question marks from the first line, saying and affirming that: All of the above will help you to know in what way "Solana's (SOL) value will continue to rise".

AT THIS MOMENT a cryptocurrency can be on the cusp and in that same second, reach the base of the iceberg.

WE MUST KEEP in mind and be very aware that there are times and seasons in which the market tends to be relatively stable, however; we cannot ignore that any economic, social, political, warlike or natural situation that may arise in society, may affect and jeopardize the behavior and the stock market index of the cryptographic network.

That is why it is compromising and embarrassing to say that yes, the value will increase and Solana (SOL) will skyrocket; everything could depend on the great upheaval that occurs at that very moment in the virtual market.

If the decision, according to the evolution that has manifested the behavior and growth of the price of Solana (SOL), is to invest a certain amount of money, it is really important to begin to constantly monitor how your currency behaves and any kind of movement inherent to the platform, Blockchain, Apps, capitalization, and everything that means numerical and dynamic activity in the ecosystem of the cryptographic network. Here it is appropriate to rely on the various opinions and analyses that are published and issued by professionals and experts, capable of issuing predictions, quite close to the facts and reality.

A long-term prediction is hesitant and difficult to sustain, however, it is a social phenomenon that users tend to applaud. Of all the people who invest in cryptocurrencies, the majority yearn to ensure a long-term, sustainable investment of capital and resources. Living every moment attentive, pending, up to date with the daily movement or course of a virtual currency, could look like a stressful dynamic for some (the majority), but fascinating for another group (the minority); this situation can certainly lead to the decision to make a wrong move and suffer losses of resources.

If the daily agitation, the change of digits of cryptocurrencies constantly on a screen is distressing for you; then choose to make long-term investments, this option will allow you to be calmer, have more free time and study a little more the financial and mercantile activity concerning the cryptographic spectrum, of which the investor will become part of the community, the network and the virtual economic system.

Observing, listening, reading, understanding, being analytical and deciding in moments of decisive reasoning will help to make proper use of both the funds invested and the goods to be received. Always attentive to the movements of the cryptocurrency that you have decided to adopt as an investment resource. Remember, Solana (SOL) is holding and growing.

Solana's competitors

With just over a year and a half of existence in the cryptographic digital network, Solana (SOL) is already positioned in fourth place as the best coin in the world, surpassing expectations and leaving its followers, experts and forecasters surprised. It is growing in price and capitalization, getting closer every day to an interesting rival. And when we say "rival", we know that it is not the opponent to be defeated; we are referring to the healthy and professional capacity to grow, develop and improve in structure and, in principle, to compete against oneself, seeking to be better and better.

Then, when subjective self-improvement begins to bear fruit, an external energy begins to transform and, when those around us perceive it and notice changes of importance and interest, sometimes a battle is unleashed to conquer or maintain a position, a property or a status. It is inevitable that we allow ourselves to let lose or let win without doing anything. Everything in life is a matter of attitude and survival, feeling or actually being the fittest. The real answer and result to a situation of rivalry is in the way a race, a competition, is managed.

In daily life we compete for everything and against everything, since life itself does not demand to be competent, and by being competent; we must also be fair and recognize in which or which moment is the right one to give way to the relay, to new energies and ideas, accepting and adapting to the changes with the best disposition.

When a human or material resource appears on the life scene with a fresh, new, energetic image, with disposition, entrepreneurial spirit, sense of collaboration, with new contributions and feasible and effective proposals; a race will be generated to try to overcome all this. Now, if the race is carried out in a fair, enthusiastic way, with the best compliance with rules, guidelines and regulations; all competitors will see only one winner, the one who will become champion, will be welcomed by all, applauded, recognized; and his strategy of struggle will be admired and worthy of imitation. All will be willing to be more and more capable, productive and convinced to act for the common good and to prepare themselves constantly.

We take this analogy to the cryptographic network and we imagine thousands of currencies "rolling" along the highway of digital finance, buying, selling, exchanging, etc. and just like a marathon; many are left on the road, while others remain steady, with the only difference that as they advance, they are sowing and leaving contributions in favor of those who still remain in the struggle and for themselves.

How many times do we have to pass through the same place again and again in the same competition, how many times does the striker of a soccer team face the opponent's goal in the first 45 minutes of the game? Analyzing the example of the race and interpreting the questions, it is easy to understand that a cryptocurrency will be able to pass several times through the same position in the market ranking, it is on its developers and all its participants to achieve for it climbing with all possible momentum. Let's not say that all digital currencies want to become Bitcoin (BTC), but they surely want to dream of being number 1.

So from there, let's see who are the competitors of Solana (SOL) or against what or who competes this platform that, in the last hours of the second week of November 2021, impresses with its climbing position among the top four.

Already for the last quarter of the year 2021, we have seen some surprising movements around the coexistence that has marked the market activity of the most prominent cryptocurrencies and that keeps in vigil the participants of the network, capturing all their attention and arousing more concern in the investors of the cryptoverse that remains in transforming activity.

Faced with this situation, others; the global markets react by asking themselves a series of questions, trying to answer what is going on, what are the news that are coming, why there is so much commotion, at what moment all this commotion, movements, changes began and who is the responsible or protagonist that surprisingly is contributing positively against known projects, to mention a few: Cardano (ADA), Ethereum (ETH) and Bitcoin (BTC). Well, all concerns and queries have their answer; for this case is Solana (SOL), a token that impresses in such a short time has reached an impressive growth of 8,600% for the year 2021 and that in the Top 10 of the best virtual currencies by market capitalization, surpassing itself, to reach an excellent fourth place, with just over 74 billion US dollars in its value and price above 247.00 US dollars. A surprising move.

If we focus on one of the most important financial web portals in the world and review their lists, we are going to find that the Solana token (SOL) is the cryptoasset of more evolution and higher growth during the year 2021, surpassing a little more than 20 times the expansion rate of Ether, the unit that represents the Ethereum platform (ETH) and in more than 110 times the expansion rate of Bitcoin (BTC).

By last September the growth of Solana (SOL) was 400%, around this situation and a relevant market persuasion, experts and insiders, pointed towards the SOL token, claiming that the Solana Blockchain (SOL) would be too close to impose itself over Ethereum (ETH), a close competitor, although having Binance in the way. The fourth place that Solana (SOL) occupies today, imbues it with solidity and robustness, gives confidence and optimism to its followers, while it strengthens as a platform at a general level.

Solana (SOL) was born with a purpose; and that purpose is to become an alternative and an option that satisfies great needs of the network and that this allows it to become the second best cryptocurrency in the ecosystem, by market capitalization. In this is immersed a great objective and of which we do not doubt at all, the evidence proves it and these evidences are price, capitalization and position.

In addition to this, we must also recognize the efficiency with which this platform operates compared to other Blockchain that have been used as references for the creation of new decentralized solutions, besides being a fast network, it has an extreme adaptability capacity. All this makes it gain important competitors, call one of them:

ETHEREUM (ETH).

Solana (SOL) has a very valuable quality of sustenance as a very well built base or structure, and it is which cornerstone; the Solana (SOL) project has a very well elaborated configuration that allows it to stand out among all at the time of providing solutions to certain problems or bottlenecks that arise even within the Ethereum (ETH) Blockchain that sometimes hinders its normal development in the real world.

Solana (SOL) has such a great and powerful resource to its credit that it is considered to be its great asset. It is about providing a solution to the well-known "Blockchain Trilemma". That is, not being able to accomplish three things at the same time. These three elements of the trilemma are:

SECURITY - PERFORMANCE - DECENTRALIZATION.

THE DEVELOPMENT OF A BLOCKCHAIN, capable of solving this controversial contradiction and that has the capacity to bring feasible applications to the real world, in particular to "Decentralized Finance" (DeFi), in which there were many proposals from other platforms that offered a way out, but did not provide them or failed to comply and rivaled Ethereum's Ether (ETH) after this goal, and at the least expected moment, came to the cryptographic network by Solana (SOL) the solution to an issue that seemed far away in time.

The scalability of Solana (SOL) is one of its most relevant features as a project, something that represents a serious problem quite common and that other Blockchain platforms must face. To this we must necessarily add the extraordinary speed it possesses and the ability to process up to 50,000 transactions per second, making it the most advanced network at this stage and with great technological changes.

All this has made Solana (SOL) take away the dream of Ethereum (ETH) developers and its closest neighbors in the ranking of the best cryptocurrencies and also arouse great interests and concerns in institutional organizations and individual investors, who are confident that there will be a promising future for Solana (SOL), to which we are convinced; will continue to add more and valuable prospects that by their confidence and investment, will make a new Boom! in favor of Solana (SOL), whose competitors will be forced to innovate.

Specialists, experts and experts in the field, converge on the same point, highlighting almost in unison that there is an exclusive and decisive feature, which makes Solana (SOL) unique in such condition, and is the implementation of a new typology or genealogy for the verification of its nodes, inspired by a system of "Proof of Stake" (PoS) due and carefully endorsed that gives rise to a mix of consensus protocol that is based on the historical and chronological aspect of the network. The token has developed a new complementary model for unique and special verification that has been called "Proof of History" (PoH), offering the most scalable possibilities in the crypto ecosystem, "Proof of Work" (PoW) style. PoH is a real time guarantee on events and happenings that occur second by second in the network.

An additional point of pleasure is that this new consensus protocol has been effective in reducing transaction costs on the network, i.e., that less is being invested in terms of GAS fees. In essence and in summary, we have found in front of us a highly efficient Blockchain, with necessary resources for the resolution of online problems, bandwidth inequalities between participants, among others; thanks to achieve a reasonable cost reduction, a great and wonderful speed, and for main detail; the creation of its "Proof of History" (PoH) system, allowing effective communication between the nodes of the Blockchain or blockchain.

Despite the fact that Solana (SOL) differs from the others for being such a promising platform, specialists in the digital community keep alive the uncertainty about whether, Solana (SOL) will finally become a declared competitor for Ethereum (ETH), imposing itself over it and other cryptocurrencies, or the equation will be reversed; and it will be Solana (SOL) to which a group of competitors will be created that also consolidate in Blockchain with applications to real life, as we know it. All of them would be practically forced to surpass the entire architecture that Solana (SOL) has built to date.

In this climate of major changes, rapid development and stiff competition, we find it somewhat difficult to believe that a winner will emerge from among the cryptocurrencies that exist today, or that, on the contrary, a new Blockchain will appear in the coming days, weeks, months or years. That is why we must be vigilant and up to date with everything that happens on the network or be informed of the most relevant.

There are many opinions on the subject of competition to and from Solana (SOL). And we think that it is not a competition to win or defeat, we do not consider a competition that leaves one of the parties out of the game, nor that between the competitors there are injured parties. As participants of the digital economic system, we bet on a competition to give more every day, to sediment knowledge, development programs; we focus on a competition of construction and improvement, a battle in which one of the parties sees the best of the other, and contribute with some improvement or effective complement.

Solana (SOL) enjoys having stigmatized its own differentiating characteristics that make it prevail over the others, and we mention some of them:

It is a Blockchain with the highest processing capacity compared to other Blockchains.

- Every 400 milliseconds, it generates the creation of a block. Number one: Bitcoin (BTC) creates a block every 10 minutes, while Ethereum does it in 20 seconds.

- Solana (SOL) transaction fees manage to be reduced to 0.000005 SOL, an estimated 0.00065 US cents.
- There is no need to move to the Second Layer at all. This eliminates the risk of being exposed to the massive exit conflict, a situation that, on the contrary, affects other Blockchains.
- There is absolutely no need for any kind of fragmentation of the Blockchain into parts, a proposal that Ethereum 2.0 makes and that Solana (SOL) does not need.

SOLANA (SOL) WAS DEVELOPED since 2017, but its activity in the cryptographic network began in 2020 and since March of that year it has been operating in its MainNet Beta. To date, it still does not have a sufficiently clear, defined and detailed roadmap, which brings as a consequence, that there is no precise information establishing a date until which it will abandon the operation system or application in Beta mode. Prior to this, Anatoly Yakovenko assures the community that the next important step that he wishes to give to Solana (SOL) is the incorporation and affiliation of no less than 1 billion new users. A sufficiently ambitious goal, which in current conditions is not difficult to achieve if we evaluate the historical growth of the token, the motivation and the recruitment of its first followers.

Yakovenko is a character of excellent public relations, of easy entry to groups and with socialization strategies that have allowed him multiple opportunities. And if he also competes, against himself, to give Solana (SOL) a greater number of followers in favor of its growth both in human and economic resources that will result in materials; let's be sure and let's guarantee that he will do so. We are convinced that the competitive projects of Solana (SOL), will start by improving at home and from each one, then to the platform and from there to the whole ecosystem. This and much more will be the Solana of the future, we see it starting in the short term.

Competition, competitors; projects, developments; supply,

demand. To this we add experience and commitment. Solana (SOL) is transforming the digital network from deep inside and the community supports it. More than competing Solana (SOL) is about surrounding itself with competitors; the ecosystem deserves a competition in which the opponents enter the arena to fight, but armed with the most effective and timely solutions.

6

THE BEST PROJECTS DEVELOPED IN SOLANA

I f we talk about popularity, notoriety and cryptographic reputation, we definitely cannot leave aside the most mediatic cryptocurrency in the digital ecosystem. Solana (SOL) is a mandatory topic of conversation, and not only for its price, market capitalization, speed and scalability, for its contribution of great first-line computational solutions or for being the fourth best currency in the world and with the highest overall growth; but also for the structure that is behind the scenes, which complements a wonderful compendium of unique qualities and that all are in the same place, in the same Blockchain, it is not necessary to look in others what you get in one.

As a result of this, there are numerous programs, plans and projects that Solana (SOL) is developing to execute and implement, serving the token and the user community. Many projects developed in Solana (SOL) found there, the icing on the cake. A suitable software, a customized environment, appropriate protocols, immediate responses and in essence; the place to act with alternative freedom based on a high-level Blockchain, supported by a multidisciplinary staff of developers dedicated to ensure the integrity of Solana (SOL) for its permanence in the network.

Below, we will present only some of the many projects developed in the Solana (SOL) network, which you will know and we invite you to deepen in them and others, checking the openness that this Blockchain has in favor of the cryptographic ecosystem.

Only1 (LIKE)

It is a project that is focused on providing a new option as a platform in the best style of social network RRSS completely decentralized, which aims to benefit from the great potential inherent in the "Non Fungible Tokens" (NFT) and added to a set of primacies and opportunities that make available the known "Decentralized Finance" (Decentralized Finance - DeFi). This project seeks to achieve a sustainable development with certain similarities to the already known social networks RRSS known and that are centralized. Only1 (LIKE) is a socialization platform in which its users will need to create their public profile through a KYC validation, then generate the desired content in NFT format, through a mechanism known as Genesis process.

Once the community is created, followers or fans of the profile begin to be obtained, these followers of the content creator, after interacting in the RRSS social network, will be able to buy or acquire the content of their interest, with the native token of the platform called Like. It is important to note that followers have the freedom to staking in the profiles of content generators or creators, this is a very important strategy, as it allows creators to give rewards to their followers, product of their own earnings.

ONLYI (LIKE) IS a practical interactive demonstration where the Win-Win philosophy is demonstrated 100%, here; if they want, everyone wins.

AN ADDITIONAL AND interesting fact is that Onlyi (LIKE) users can request as a rental the content published by any of the creators followed by them, then; and from the same the user can use it and thus also have the possibility to generate or create their own content, based on the basis established in the profile of another creator. This modality is ideal to extend the dissemination of content and the credit of the participants who create digital material that is easy to negotiate and commercialize. It is a very attractive and fun way to take the best advantage of the trend that the RRSS social network has as a quality to earn profits, from which the original creator will receive the corresponding royalties from the publication. One more way to be close and connected between the creator and his followers.

MoonLana (MOLA)

It is also a decentralized project, self-described as a community platform project and which the vast majority identifies as the Meme Coin platform and second generation. To know if it is indeed a Meme Coin, it is convenient to review its characteristics and those aspects that could well be similar or with great similarity to those that are in essence a MemeCoin.

Let's take a look at the following information about the characteristics of accounts with MemeCoin features.

SUPPLY:

Although its amount is not similar to that of other projects, it is quite high. It is really huge and very high, preventing the token from increasing its price in a considerable and representative way; it is 4,000,000,000,000,000,000 billion tokens.

PRICE: It is characterized by containing a high amount of zeros in front, something quite common in different meme projects. Here applies a purely psychological reason of intentions and purposes that generally affects new investors, making them believe that the price is really low; creating the false illusion that if at some point, the price of the project would reach the value of 1.00 US dollar, their investment would make them millionaires.

MARKETING: The advertising and marketing plans of this project are really fascinating, they have a wonderful style and powerful campaigns are designed; a very well managed tool that allows the consolidation of a large and quite strong community. An example of this is Shiba Inu, whose marketing plan continues to give excellent results.

This project turns out to be very interesting and has a series of characteristics that differentiate it from the others:

IT SELF-MANAGES ITS EXCHANGE: MoonLana (MOLA), develops its own decentralized exchange program, within which negotiations are made in terms of NFT, music, logos and other assets of Blockchain importance for this market. To acquire these assets, one must interact with their native token.

GAME: We already know what has a game, however, this is kept in reserve and there are no descriptive details about it.

· · ·

Tools: Registered under the name of LanaTools, it has its own platform. It offers some interesting advantages such as highlighted price alerts, new project tracking and asset charts among a variety of highlights.

Mango (MNGO)

In this case we are talking about a project belonging to a "Decentralized Autonomous Organization" (DAO), which aims to create a complete and fully integrated crypto market platform that meets all the requirements that the network and the current web demand. It is conceived as one of the most ambitious digital projects possible, seeking to become the gem of the virtual ecosystem.

Mango (MNGO) is already defined and is a decentralized crypto-asset exchange and marketplace platform just like a DEX (Decentralized Exchange). Mango (MNGO) turns out to be much more complete, since it gives us the freedom to place orders at the price you want to buy, is open to leverage, activates price alerts; among other functions. We can say that Mango (MNGO) is a perfect fusion of CEX (Centralized Exchange) and DEX (Decentralized Exchange).

About Mango (MNGO), it is important to consider:

Supply: Its monumental supply, as it has a minimum circulation of 1,000,000,000,000 and a maximum circulation of 10,000,000,000,000. This will make it impossible for the asset to reach a higher and higher price, a situation not very well seen by current and new investors.

Where to buy: Due to the novelty of the project, it is only possible to buy through FTX.

. . .

PASSIVE INCOME: It is possible to receive payments and profits, but only in a passive way, granting loans from the same platform.

BACKING: This project has the backing and support of the Alameda Research organization.

TREND: Given its new founding date, it is not yet possible to determine the trend that the project may have. The invitation is to make staggered purchases and thus enter them.

Now, other large and outstanding projects to highlight in Solana (SOL), which have represented portentous income, are Grape Protocol, which we talked about in detail in chapter 1 of this work, which managed to raise 600,000 US dollars. On the other hand, we have Parrot Protocol, which managed to raise more than US$69 million as part of an initial proposal for the DEX (Decentralized Exchange) platform. Parrot Protocol counted among its group of investors renowned entities, including Alameda Research, QTUM VC. Parrot and Simo Global Capital.

In contrast to Grape Protocol, QTUM VC. Parrot is based on the PAI stablecoin, although to process its "Initial Decentralized Exchange Offering" (Initial DEX Offering - IDO), Parrot decided to create and publish its native token and release it under the name of PRT, allowing users of the Blockchain to make withdrawals of their income without having to affect the resources of the "Yield Farms".

Larix is another of the projects developed in Solana. The first record of this development is that its estimated value, in just three days, skyrocketed from US$1.7 million to US$119 million. Huobi Global and Polygon, together with the Solana network were its first investors.

The last quarter of 2021 has been encouraging for Solana (SOL) in every way. Having reached a position of such importance as the fourth best cryptocurrency in the world, has generated buzz inside and outside the network, its price, although with slight drops; possesses high levels of growth. The firm consolidation of its computational architecture and the solution tools from its Blockchain, among its many contributions, open the way to continue growing. And as followers, users and prospects; we assure that its number of customers and direct participants will increase, according to Yakovenko's desire; to grow his project, and from Solana (SOL), to support the Solana Foundation, training and supporting the international community with educational programs.

The dynamic continues, the network shakes and Solana (SOL), must bet to continue in unstoppable flight, crossing borders that strengthen and consolidate the financial digital ecosystem.

The rise of NFTs in Solana

Nowadays we have been immersed more frequently in a world of relationships and activities at a distance, we live a new normality and this includes online interaction, from where the world dynamics has generated great changes.

Between these and other phenomena, we go straight to the movements and activities of the cryptoverse, and there we find Solana (SOL) and at the same time, a series of projects, developments, processes, protocols and Apps with updated and novel features; But there is a particular event and impact, the phenomenon of the "Non Fungible Tokens" (NFT), which in certain and certain moments reaches very high temperature levels from the Ethereum Blockchain (ETH) but now they pass to Solana (SOL). There are numerous projects of "Non Fungible Tokens" (NFT) that are beginning to arise and to conform within Solana (SOL), thanks to the benefits and facilities provided by the Blockchain.

The network has a high-end and open source Blockchain that provides great scalability and, among many features, has the ability to support Smart Contracts. Solana (SOL) provides us with a decentralized, highly scalable platform that replaces the consensus mechanism with its own Proof of History (PoH) consensus protocol.

Solana (SOL) uses the hash of the final transaction to create the hash of the next transaction. This is known as clear transaction order, producing a long chain of transactions. This process automatically eliminates the TimeStamp, an unavoidable mechanism for Bitcoin (BTC) and Ethereum (ETH).

Let's learn a little more about Non Fungible Tokens (NFT) This is the name given to non-divisible tokens, which are collectible and stored on the Blockchain. The "Non Fungible Tokens" (NFT) store all the data of the creator, the characteristics of the token and the information of its holder. These steps are fundamental in order to avoid any type of forgery and guarantee a unique element.

Today, the "Non Fungible Tokens" (NFT) are very popular, allowing to consolidate a commercial structure of millions and millions of US dollars. All the information corresponding to the "Non Fungible Tokens" (NFT), is kept available and protected, avoiding its forgery or theft.

Only until a few weeks ago, Non Fungible Tokens (NFT) were overflowing the Ethereum (ETH) cup, but the fact of having such high commissions motivated new actions in the community. Once Solana (SOL) made its appearance, an effect was generated through which many creators and developers began to devise solutions in favor of Non Fungible Tokens (NFT) with the support of the Solana (SOL) Blockchain. An ultra-fast process and the creation of the cheapest Non Fungible Tokens (NFT) were enough to experience the great exodus to Solana (SOL), provoked by the disadvantages that other platforms proved, and against which there was nothing to do. This situation or condition remains.

There is a huge number of Non Fungible Token (NFT) stores and active and developing games that are going at an unstoppable pace, thanks to Solana (SOL). Let's keep in mind that this Blockchain has not yet reached two years of activity, which is why it has a small number of projects developed on it.

Currently, a small number of "Non Fungible Tokens" (NFT) projects are registered on the Solana (SOL) platform, and many of those that exist are not yet fully operational or are in a non-operational phase. The projects themselves, are few, this is because the vast majority are still using the Ethereum Blockchain The "Non Fungible Tokens" (Non Fungible Tokens - NFT), receive a lot of criticism, which revolve around the indiscriminate duplication of large Ethereum (ETH) projects. There are also those who make their criticisms about Solana's team of external developers (SOL), insisting that they perform CopyCat (token copying) of Non Fungible Tokens (NFT). It should be made clear that this probable copying of NFT is not isolated, as for last March, an irregular situation by Binance Smart Chain in projects such as Euler Beats or Crypto Punks, "Non Fungible Tokens" (Non Fungible Tokens - NFT) of Ethereum were replicated.

This is a situation, if somewhat irregular; it is considered "something more or less normal", due to the fact that certain groups of developers take the opportunity to "cash out".

A significant number of participants ask Solana (SOL) to make efforts to awaken originality and creativity, while others see with good eyes the issue of migrating to Solana (SOL), because in this way the creators of "Non Fungible Tokens" (NFT) and investors are authorized to create their tokens, market them and offer them through low commissions in Ethereum (ETH).

Some types of Non Fungible Tokens (NFT) projects in Solana that can stand out, have already done so or will disappear.

Solanart

It is a Non Fungible Tokens (NFT) marketplace with functionality from the Solana Blockchain (SOL), providing its participants with a space for the purchase and sale of Non Fungible Tokens (NFT) practical and simple enough. It has been conceived under the image of a MarketPlace In Solanart the "Non Fungible Tokens" (NFT) are not stored, what is done is to generate a temporary account and also generate a smart contract or smartcontract with the token of the Solana Blockchain (SOL) and its price.

SOLANIA:

A very unusual "Non Fungible Tokens" (NFT) project in which planets with very unique characteristics are traded. On one occasion, 10,000 unique planets were put on initial pre-sale and those that did not sell were destroyed. Solania managed to sell all the initial collectible planets in its catalog. At the moment there are no details about this project.

FTX:

It is an Exchange that offers a section of "Non Fungible Tokens" (Non Fungible Tokens - NFT), based on the Solana (SOL) and Ethereum (ETH) Blockchain. In FTX we are given the possibility to create and trade Non Fungible Tokens (NFT). The price for each NFT is 10 US dollars. When this platform was opened to the public, it suffered a severe spam attack. As a result, the creation price went from 10 to 500 US dollars per unit.

SOLANIMALS:

This is an interesting project that proposes the breeding of animals, something like an adaptation of the famous CryptoKitties. It is currently out of service due to reconstruction.

PANDA FRATERNITY:

This is another project that promotes animal affection. It is about collecting panda bears in the form of "Non Fungible Tokens" (NFT) that conform and make life in an animal fraternity. It consists of issuing 10,000 pandas in the initial phase to finance the project. 500 pandas were issued in "Non Fungible Tokens" (NFT), after a pre-sale process, leaving 9,500 for open trading to the public. Phase date: September 11, 2021.

METAMARKET:

This is a Decentralized Exchange (DEX), which is based on Solana Serum (SOL) and includes a Non Fungible Tokens (NFT) store. A point of interest with this project is that it is on GitHub, as an open source application, in base format for developers.

SWANLANA:

Among the most attractive projects that we will find in Solana (SOL), Swanlana is one of them. All this because it is a "Decentralized Exchange" (DEX), which will have a section for "Non Fungible Tokens" (NFT) plus the implementation of a social network RRSS related to Solana (SOL). Although it is still under construction, the network awaits its launch with much excitement and enthusiasm.

NINJA PROTOCOL:

In the network we find a wide variety of markets. From marketing to sell, buy and create "Non Fungible Tokens" (NFT), to random creation of NFT. This project, called Ninja Protocol, is a multiplayer game that will obtain NFT, something that has recently become more and more common. This game project takes us on a journey to the times of samurai soldiers in the era of the Shoguns. At the moment information is scarce and the project is in the development phase.

CIRCLEPOD:

Due to the confinement resulting from COVID-19, we found ourselves, and still are, working from home. For this reason, a number of platforms have appeared for online and live transmissions, with the intention of maintaining active communication and generating content of global interest. Circlepod, is presented as an option and a resource for creation and generation of next generation content within the Solana Blockchain (SOL), which incorporates "Non Fungible Tokens" (NFT). For its developers, it will be effective and secure connection and communication between participants. This project includes artificial intelligence.

THE DEVELOPERS of the Solana Blockchain (SOL), are in the initial phase, remember that the Solana MainNet (SOL) is still in beta mode, i.e. in the initial process. Many of the aforementioned projects appeared during the second half of the year 2021, so, there are many projects that will be added. Although many of them seem quite trivial, nothing relevant; others appear to be really interesting. As we go along, we will see how the incursion of new projects and proposals for "Non Fungible Tokens" (NFT), based on Solana (SOL), will be managed and completed.

The future of Solana (Roadmap)

Since 2017 Anatoly Yakovenko started to develop what to this day is called Solana (SOL). Since March 2020, the platform has been operating in the Beta format of its MainNet. An aspect of extreme importance for everyone is that Solana (SOL) does not have a RoadMap, it lacks this valuable resource, and it is obvious that therefore we do not know, nor do we have precise information that tells us, until when Solana (SOL) will continue in Beta format, that is to say, until what day it will operate from the MainNet. For the time being, and given the situation of not managing these small details, we will remain satisfied with the data and information that we continue to receive from its platform and communication channels.

In a press release published last June, the CEO of Solana (SOL), Anatoly Yakovenko, made it known that "the next step is the incorporation of one billion users". Yakovenko, as a spokesman and in the best RoadMap style, announced what would be Solana's (SOL) next conquest. There were no further comments, no questions; only the notification of the sanitized ambition of wanting to have a large community that, undoubtedly, will enjoy the great benefits of being part of this Blockchain that grows day by day in price, value, market capitalization, scalability, popularity and the number 4 position as the best cryptocurrency in the world.

Mentioning scalability, it is noteworthy that the proposal made by solana, which consists in guaranteeing scalability, is interesting and promising enough. The combination of its consensus protocol "Proof of History" (PoH) with the "Proof of Stake" (PoS), has shown surprising results of security and potentiality. This condition will serve as an attraction for many other projects moving along the same line, in order to also use this combination. However, it is important to always keep in mind that ups and downs in a cryptographic project are part of its existence.

Solana (SOL) has generated a resounding impact across the globe with its presence and participation in the market and with its novel management operating system for its Blockchain. The speed of Solana (SOL) in its transactions is a key feature that draws attention and attracts interest in the network, an aspect that is simply liked in the digital ecosystem.

This whole idea about a new fast and efficient cryptocurrency, was well thought out for 2017, three years of design, planning and development; a new financial digital alternative was coming out to the crypto market that, in less than two years of active and commercial life, has turned third parties upside down.

Now, about the future of Solana (SOL), will it be only the speed that will make its difference? Let's remember that we are talking about a virtual currency that is practically a phenomenon on the network. From it, there are many projects that are supported and generated as a domino effect that transmits a message without words, where only the actions and satisfactions do the work to Solana (SOL). Its cooperative and transforming presence, in addition to a stable structure in constant revision, guarantee a stable and constructive present, the basis for a productive future and a globalized presence as an advanced Blockchain, development, growth and conviction in order to maintain and surpass itself.

With extreme speed, Solana (SOL), the token that was created with the objective of sustaining its own platform, suddenly begins to grow, to obtain more value and as soon as the circumstances conspire in its favor, it becomes one of the powerful digital currencies in the world, of course; respecting its distances with Ethereum (ETH) and Bitcoin (BTC). Solana (SOL) increases its market capitalization and price, in what many of us consider a record, just a few months after its release.

Notably, Solana (SOL) managed to outperform coins such as Dogecoin (DOGE), Polkadot (DOT) and Shiba Inu (SHIB), very quickly.

With the greatest of respect, we have witnessed the amazing way in which Solana (SOL), in the best parkour style, has had a huge climb, but yes; very reserved, perhaps having some very well kept secrets and that perhaps, Yakovenko himself one day will share for the learning of others. In these conditions, unfortunately anything goes; from good to cruel comments, because in Solana (SOL) there is still an important level of reserve, which we can understand, accept and comprehend.

In the immediate, short-term future, we are confident that Solana (SOL) will maintain its style, rhythm and operating scheme. Its behavior promises modest, and perhaps healthy competition. From the most technological point of view, it will continue its own attitude as any other cryptocurrency, taking care of its decentralized network, vigilant of its complex software system; something that has radically distinguished it from the rest of the Blockchains for other digital currencies.

One way to be guaranteed a stable future is to have confidence in its structure and design architecture. Solana (SOL) has been known as the currency that competes with Ethereum (ETH), and the mere fact of having a network with a strictly organized recording system and chronological order of events that surpasses consensus and Blockchain protocols such as Bitcoin (BTC), makes it feel secure and optimistic. On the other hand, each and every one of its transactions contains detailed temporal information, providing a unique facility and optimal use of time for an exclusive performance in the creation of a complete blockchain, for which it has a multi plexing system by fraction of time.

Thanks to the use of the SHA-256 algorithm that was created by Bitcoin (BTC), Yakovenko has designed the famous "Cryptographic Clock" that allows reporting with total accuracy, the exact time in which a transaction or event occurs in the Blockchain. It is a clock that avoids the issuance of transactions with erroneous or even false information and does not require the intervention of third parties, where validators do not depend on communicating with each other to obtain chronological information of activities in the network.

Time is relentless, it does not stop, it does not go backwards, its path is constant, just like the Blockchain, from where Solana (SOL), also seeks to respect time, that of its and its due operations, that of its developers, that of its work team, that of its customers, and in general that of the entire network and different platforms that make life an economic structure that benefits and activates the different markets and active commercial and financial styles.

Solana (SOL) is a futuristic currency that, although we are still in debt and awaiting its Roadmap and continues to operate in beta format from its MainNet, it has a promising future, hoping to maintain the stability and growth demonstrated in less than two years of existence, which so far has given much to talk about and a lot of details to learn.

7

GENERATING PASSIVE INCOME WITH SOLANA (SOL) USING OTHER CRYPTOCURRENCIES

A s you may have noticed throughout the development of the book, currently there are several ways to generate money with cryptocurrencies, there are many opportunities. While there are some that are more risky (and depend on your ability) such as trading, DeFi platforms, etc, there are others that are more recommended and less risky, such as Hodl (hold) of a cryptocurrency and wait for its price to rise, although this earning model is absolutely passive and speculative, as it is a long-term strategy, we have other strategies that can also help you generate passive income, as is the strategy that I will present below.

This strategy has existed for many years, it is widely used by banks today, although in a higher percentage of profit, this is to generate interest with your assets.

In the world of cryptocurrencies this modality already exists and is led by one of the most reliable companies in the environment: BlockFi, which is backed by the Gemini exchange and people as recognized in the environment as Anthony Pompliano.

BlockFi allows us to transfer our funds to the platform and generate an annual interest that goes from 6% (for cryptocurrencies such as Bitcoin) or almost 10% with stablecoins (which are cryptocurrencies that are 1 to 1 with the dollar, such as USDT and USDC to name a few).

If you are interested in this modality, you can open a BlockFi account at the following link and earn $250 worth of Bitcoin for free:

Get your BONUS on BlockFi here

IN CASE you are reading this book in print version you can scan the following QR code with your cell phone:

8

THE MOST IMPORTANT THINGS TO KEEP IN MIND WITH SOLANA

To conclude this book, I would like to thank you for taking the time to read it, I wanted to clarify a few things before finishing.

Many people have tried dabbling in cryptocurrencies, some with success others with moderate results, but all with results in the end, the important thing is that you keep in mind that the cryptocurrency market is a highly manipulated market, which is why I recommend that you always pay attention to the indicators that you can see in TradingView, see the signals it sends you, continue learning about trading, if you are interested you can dedicate yourself to them, but if not you can dedicate yourself to do HODL (the meaning of this within the Cryptocurrencies is related to buy coins when there is a significant decline (for example if Bitcoin is at $58000 and drops to $36500 that's where you buy and go buying as it goes down, never when it goes up, this is known as Dollar Cost Averaging is a strategy widely used in the trading environment) and keep those cryptocurrencies for years until they double, triple or quadruple their value, it is not uncommon in the environment, as well have done those early adopters who bought Bitcoin when it was worth $0.006 cents, did HODL for 14 years and when Bitcoin reached its all-time high of $20,000 dollars in 2017 and $60,000 in 2021, sold everything and became millionaires. But as always, choose the method you like best and follow it at your own risk.

Finally, I would like to know your comments to continue to nurture this book and to help many more people, for them would you help us by leaving a review of this book, in order to continue providing great books to you, my readers, which I appreciate very much.

LINKS **for you**

Check crypto prices here:
https://coinmarketcap.com/
Get free Bitcoin:
Get free bitcoin here
Get your BlockFi bonus here:
https://blockfi.com/?ref=76971ae9

Trading crypto:

Binance

Bitmex

Buy Crypto:

Coinbase

CEX.IO

Changally

Localbitcoins

Donde guardar tus criptomonedas:

Get the Trezor Model T here

Get the Trezor Model ONE here

Get a Ledger Nano S here

More trading tools at:

www.TradingView.com

Best regards
Sebastian Andres

9

DO YOU WANT TO FURTHER DEEPEN YOUR KNOWLEDGE?

I f you found this book very useful, let me tell you that this book is part of the collection "Criptomonedas en Español" where we want to transmit all the current education and information based on the most traded and known cryptocurrencies (the books will be updated every year as progress is made).

- Volume 1: **Bitcoin in a Nutshell**
- Volume 2: **Ethereum in a Nutshell**
- Volume 3: **Dogecoin in a Nutshell**
- Volume 4: **Cardano in a Nutshell**
- Volume 5: **Solana in a Nutshell**